TRAUMA
from the INSIDE OUT

A Psychotherapist and Her
Client Share Both Sides of a Healing Journey

SUSAN H. BOWKER, MSW, LCSW
ELIZABETH O'MALLEY, PsyD

TRAUMA FROM THE INSIDE OUT
Susan H. Bowker, MSW, LCSW
Elizabeth O'Malley, PsyD
©2017 All Rights Reserved.

ISBN-13: 978-0692831502
ISBN-10: 0692831509

design: t. nuccio/nucciocreative

Acknowledgments

Susan Bowker

First, I must offer my deepest thanks to my co-writer, who had both the willingness and drive to do the work in therapy that asked so much of her, and then the courage to revisit years of her traumatic memories from both her childhood and her work in therapy with me to write this book. I will forever be grateful for her belief in what we learned together and for her determination to share it with others despite the personal cost.

I also wish to acknowledge the ongoing support of my peer supervision group who were with me during my work with Elizabeth and served as early readers of this book: Dr. Vicki Seglin, Dr. Lynne Simon and Cynthia Ashton. Their support and feedback was invaluable. Special thanks to Dr. June Terpstra, who walked with me through a final edit, providing critical analysis, insight and an unerring belief in the project.

Thanks, too, to our editor, Elizabeth Crown, who not only made sense of our writing, but who has consistently believed in this project.

Final thanks go to my husband, Bob, whose love and encouragement have been the fuel for this project. I could not have done it without him.

Elizabeth O'Malley*

Working through severe trauma is messy, ugly and unpredictable. Thank you, Sue, for staying by my side through such a complicated and pain-filled process. I couldn't have continued through that process without your dedication to my healing.

I dedicate this book to all trauma survivors who are feeling hopeless and for those therapists and other healers who walk by their sides. Survivors, know that you do not have to be alone in your struggles.

My support team included my spouse and many friends who shared their time and love through many years of what to me felt like wandering in a desert.

*Elizabeth has used a pen name to ensure privacy.

INTRODUCTION

THIS IS A BOOK written and conceived equally by two of us, Sue and Elizabeth, therapist and client, now colleagues and friends. It is the story of our time together in therapy that ultimately covered a 12-year period – a book written from both our perspectives. It is the product of countless hours spent together during therapy and as co-writers after the fact: exploring our individual experiences and articulating the factors that we ultimately believed contributed to our successful therapy experience.

Elizabeth suggested that we co-write a book when we were still in therapy, at a time when she felt the healing power of our relationship very powerfully. While we were in the depth of our work together, the idea was set aside and not discussed again for years. At times, the intensity of our therapy led each of us to think the other had given up on the book, but neither of us had. As we talked as collaborators, we realized that both of us had kept the idea of writing together in the back of our minds but felt that the work we were doing together in therapy needed our full attention.

Most books describing psychotherapy are written by clinicians. Fewer psychotherapy books are written by patients and even fewer written jointly by a therapist and his or her client. There are good reasons for this. The therapy relationship has quite clear expectations, and standard protocol expects that under normal conditions, once the therapeutic relationship ends, there is no contact between therapist and client. As clinicians (Sue is a clinical social worker and Elizabeth is a clinical psychologist), this has been our experience. The innate power differential, the ethical dilemmas and the considerable practical difficulties of shifting roles from therapist/client to any other dynamic all support marking the end of therapy as the end of the relationship.

Then why did we decide to change our client/therapist relationship when therapy concluded? Both of us believe that it was the therapeutic relationship we shared that pulled us through many extremely challenging periods and made healing possible. While therapists and teachers frequently talk about the "power of the healing relationship," the exact nature of that relationship is often left to the imagination. As teachers and supervisors of beginning therapists, we know that sharing our personal experiences as a client or therapist can be extremely helpful to students, making theory come alive and become accessible. We wanted to write this book because we believed the story about our therapy could illustrate a therapeutic relationship that allowed for successful healing from trauma.

ELIZABETH'S PERSPECTIVE

My experience with Sue had confirmed beliefs that were central to my understanding of therapy and I wanted to share our therapy story as a way of illustrating those beliefs. While my training as a clinical psychologist has included significant study in providing several different kinds of psychotherapy, I have come to believe that a therapeutic relationship that is genuine, honest and collaborative is the most critical part of a healing process. What is most important to me is the therapist's ability to stay in a person's frame of reference as much as possible, emphasizing the individuality of the person without relying on techniques, interpretations, diagnostic labels or a workbook.

One of those central beliefs is the importance of letting the client determine the agenda. I had been in therapy a few times before to deal with trauma and found the experiences helpful, but nothing compared to the level of freedom I experienced with Sue as new memories of extreme abuse surfaced. When I couldn't speak about the overwhelming fears I faced, I was free to tell my story in whatever way I could, including using nonverbal activities. Playing with GI Joes, building houses with Legos and scanning the therapy room with a Star Trek "tricorder" to look for bugging devices are all examples of how I was able to work meaningfully through the terrors of my memories. We could discuss whatever was most on my mind at that moment, regardless of what we had worked on in the prior session. When things were going well between us, this dynamic gave me the momentum to tackle the memories that continued to hit me in waves. When things were very difficult between us, this dynamic helped me push through my fears of my own emotions and my difficulties trusting myself or Sue and focus on our relationship.

I was working as a clinical psychologist while I was in therapy with Sue. Along with practicing psychology as an independent practitioner, I frequently found myself in workshops that discussed ways of putting more boundaries on trauma clients. I listened as other clinicians talked disparagingly about "those clients" and how difficult they were. I listened to all the methods intended to help us "manage those clients." And there I was as one of "those clients."

Sue never made me feel like "one of those clients." She seemed excited and curious about the things I would bring into a session to help me tell my story. She encouraged my exploration in whatever direction it took. Unlike many therapists who tightly control any outside connection, Sue never shamed me for needing more time to talk outside our session time. She struggled to understand why her vacations were so difficult for me and helped me to find ways of getting through them – including having sessions when we could, even when she was on vacation. It will be clear later in the book just how central this issue was for us.

SUE'S PERSPECTIVE

I shared many of Elizabeth's beliefs, and from our early discussions saw this book as an opportunity to explore and illustrate those beliefs. However, arriving at the decision to help Elizabeth finish up therapy and begin a new relationship as co-writers was more difficult. For several months, there had not been any new memories and Elizabeth felt she had regained a much higher level of competence in her world. But when Elizabeth announced that she was ready to quit and wanted to set a date, I was surprised. I thought there were still issues on the table that needed more time to address. As we talked, however, it became clear that she was indeed ready to resume her place in the world as someone far more than a "trauma client."

Transitioning from our therapy relationship to writing a book became a major part of our discussions. Everything in my training told me I was probably committing some sort of major therapist sin and that the ethics police would be at my door by morning. I don't question the need for clear boundaries, take the wisdom of so many others lightly or make rash decisions for myself. Traditional protocol calls for ending the relationship when therapy ends. No other options. The power dynamics of these therapy models keep the therapist and client in different ranks: there is an expert and there is a client. Following that model, transitioning to an equal relationship would be difficult. We had discussed collaborating on a book early in our therapy, but when the possibility of collaborating resurfaced, we each had to determine if it was possible to transition from therapist/client to colleagues and co-writers.

Yet my training in Feminist theories reminded me of a different model that allows for a less rigid understanding of the therapy relationship, emphasizing the therapist as more of an equal and less of an expert. This nonhierarchical understanding of the therapist/client relationship supports alternatives to the more traditional protocols. It allowed me to validate the powerful connection Elizabeth and I felt that went beyond the more narrowly defined therapist/client roles and consider this new relationship.

There were also selfish motivations behind considering this decision. Elizabeth and I had shared deeply. We had been through a "war" together and were bonded in a way that is hard to describe if you have not been there. I knew her before her trauma broke, and was very intrigued to get to know the articulate, bright, deep-thinking person I had known at the beginning of our work. Part of our ongoing conversation as client and therapist included our theoretical understandings of what was happening between us as client and therapist. These discussions also made me hungry to talk about our process at length and hear both her personal and clinical perspectives on our experience together.

There were also many anxieties and concerns on the other side of the decision ledger. We had this unique experience of therapy – both experiencing an intense connection with shared vulnerabilities, while not knowing each other at all. There were inherent inequities in that close relationship and lots of missing pieces. We had never shared a cup of tea, nor chatted about our families, dogs or our vacations. She knew comparably almost nothing about my life. If we continued to meet as colleagues after therapy, I knew our relationship would change, and I had to take a leap of faith to believe that we would be able to make this transition in a way that would allow for a new and different kind of collaboration.

There were deeper anxieties that came out of our experience of knowing each other during the depths of our trauma work. I have always had a hard time when therapists who work with trauma survivors talk about "vicarious trauma," the stress a healer may experience when trying to help a survivor of trauma that can lead to symptoms similar to the survivor of trauma's experience. To me, it seems a bit narcissistic to think we suffer as our clients do. Maybe it's just semantics, but I think we have to be very careful to not minimize what our clients experience with a "me too" label for ourselves.

That said, I believe we are affected by witnessing the trauma others have endured. We have our own personal demons to fight as well. For me, it was scary to begin a relationship with Elizabeth without the framework of the therapist/client boundaries. The residue I felt from deep inside trauma's belly – my version of vicarious trauma – made me perhaps unreasonably anxious about what this change might mean.

When Elizabeth was in her most vulnerable and needy state, she made it clear just how close she wanted to be with me. For example, she often had a difficult time leaving me at the end of session and she openly wished for more of a connection with me, longing to spend time together as "friends." I understood intellectually that the requests made at those times were requests made out of the panic and despair about her traumatic memories, but the memories of those requests were still with me. I was frightened that the intensity of those needs was still there, and that she might still be hoping our relationship would quickly move into "almost like family." I had to get over my fear that she was really asking for much more than she was saying and that I was likely to be put in a role of disappointing someone I knew had been disappointed in close relationships too many times. I really didn't want to be another perpetrator, at any level.

I had to battle my anxieties about the writing itself. Being in a therapeutic relationship together is very different from writing a book together. We would have to argue, hold our ground, be wrong, be edited and struggle to find the conclusions that felt right to both of us. It would be something we had not experienced together before.

I knew I had some residual shame that I would discover more failings on my part than I wanted to know. I knew we had to dig deep into a 12-year process and that we would have to look at some very difficult moments together. How would it look in retrospect? How much did I miss? How much did I "rewrite" in my head?

I also was very excited. I have always liked to write, although have never done much beyond my schooling. I was at a point in my career when it made sense to try to articulate how I thought and how my understanding of the work informed my responses to clients. I had already learned a great deal from my work with Elizabeth but believed that through writing I could learn a great deal more.

I knew it might be challenging to write about our sometimes-confusing therapy experience. I trusted that in writing this book we would both be as present, authentic and honest as we looked back with clearer eyes and tried to understand what had occurred in our frequent periods of total confusion as well as in our moments of healing.

OUR SHARED GOALS FOR WRITING THIS BOOK

From our very first conversations about wanting to co-author a book, we knew we wanted to share the story of our time together in a coherent manner that would describe very specifically one example of therapy that has traumatic events as its main focus. We had been through a lot together: Moments of seemingly endless pain, confusion and challenges to our relationship, but we had survived and Elizabeth had come out on the other side feeling that her work on her traumatic memories was done and she could create a new life without her traumatic past haunting her. It was ultimately a positive story we felt worth telling.

We recognized that our therapy relationship and our mutual willingness to transition from client and therapist to co-writers gave us an unusual opportunity. It is rare for a therapist and client to spend anywhere near the amount of time we have trying to piece together the parts of our work that were helpful and not so helpful, to share misunderstandings in retrospect and to articulate in a way that a reader could understand just what it was like to go through this experience together. We have expressed, over and over, just how surprisingly revealing it has been to go back in time and relive our therapy together.

As will become clear, we share a deep belief in the importance of the relationship in the healing process. Ours was an exceedingly complex relationship. We explored many of those complexities as therapist and client, but gained more insight after the therapy ended and could look at our relationship as colleagues and clinicians.

Our conclusions seemed rather simplistic: above all else, focusing on the relationship, being empathic and, as much as possible, staying in the moment with each other made our therapy successful. Our shared belief in the centrality of our relationship supported that success. Illustrating that process at length became our first goal.

We are aware that in reading our story some therapist readers may raise questions about the tools and techniques that are commonly used in many individual therapies with trauma survivors. These tools include a wide variety of cognitive behavioral techniques that are designed to change thinking, manage affect and decrease the symptoms of traumatic reactions. We believe that while there may be times when tools are very helpful to some clients, in our particular relationship, the risk of disempowering Elizabeth, or even shaming her, was inherent in any suggestion from Sue of a technique, tool or a direction of exploration. So, our second goal is to demonstrate a therapy that was not dependent on the most common tools, particularly if those tools are suggested by the therapist.

There were certainly tools that we did use. Elizabeth was very creative in finding nonverbal ways to express herself. Elizabeth also is an experienced meditator and used that skill when she could between sessions as a way to calm herself down. Although our therapy ultimately was successful because we had similar beliefs and theoretical orientations that grounded our conversations and placed the relationship as central, a thorough articulation of those theories is not our goal. Rather, we wanted to start, as we did in our earliest meetings as co-writers, from our experience. We are telling our story with as much clarity as possible, but without theoretical frameworks. Therefore, a third goal emerged in our agreement – to avoid "psychobabble" whenever possible, using our own terms to describe our experience, in the hope that would allow the book to remain accessible to all.

We will offer some conclusions we have drawn from our work together, but we do not claim in any way that we have a brand new theoretical framework for trauma therapy. This is not a universal template, and we do not intend for our concepts to be taken as unalterable truths that can be generalized to all trauma-based therapy.

However, we hope that the unique experience we are sharing in such detail will be helpful to many, both beginning and experienced clinicians, trauma survivors and anyone curious about the therapy experience.

CHAPTER 1

OUR JOURNEY TOGETHER

ELIZABETH'S STORY

WRITING THIS STORY was very difficult. Trying to create a coherent narrative out of incomplete and horrific memories of a crazy-making childhood is draining and challenging. I decided to give only a brief overview in the belief that it will be enough to understand the depth and complexity of my traumatic childhood history. I still have memory gaps. Over the years I have been able to corroborate many of the stories I tell, but not all. Some readers may struggle to consider my story as plausible. It was hard for me to believe it as well.

After my mother had four miscarriages and said many prayers and novenas, I was born. Eighteen months after I was born, my sister Erin joined our screwed-up, toxic family unit. My mother had two more miscarriages after my sister's birth.

From birth to age 12, I grew up geographically close to extended family on both sides. The use and abuse of alcohol pervaded these gatherings, along with merrymaking among the cousins. My parents' relationship was tumultuous. They fought with each other everywhere, but home was where the fights were truly terrifying for my sister and me. The fights were violent, and we were regularly frightened for our safety as well as that of our parents. My sister and I became adept at calling neighbors to come over to the house, knowing that our parents would stop fighting long enough to put on a show for the neighbors. Sometimes it temporarily broke the cycle.

Although Erin and I suffered most of our abuse at the hands of our father, my mother was not guilt free. She could have an awful temper as well and would hit us with brushes, clothes hangers or anything else she could reach. She yelled a lot and suffered with depression and mood swings. Now I recognize her behaviors as signs of an undiagnosed and untreated bipolar disorder. As a child, it meant living with a mother who was very unpredictable moment to moment. In her "up" moods, she could be great fun: leading us around the kitchen table singing songs and banging pots and pans. A moment later, she could be very angry and physically abusive.

My father was physically abusive also, although it was sometimes labeled as "punishment." My mother often threatened "wait until your father gets home," which resulted in a "spanking" that ranged in its severity depending on my father's mood.

Far beyond the craziness of physical violence and erratic and unavailable parenting was the consistent sexual abuse by my father. I don't remember a time when my father wasn't touching me in a sexual way. His interactions initially ranged from inappropriate and sexualized hugging with his pulling me to him in a rhythmic way, to touching my breasts and genitals. At some point while we were living in a city in California, he began raping me. He didn't care that my sister was also in the bedroom watching from her bed. Some nights he came into the room to rape my sister instead. I have no idea where my mother was or if she knew this was happening or not. We just thought she didn't care about us.

When I was in junior high school, our family moved from an urban area in California to a less-populated mountainous area. As hard as it was to deal with leaving family and friends behind, our home life also degenerated as my mother began a job that required her to be away from home more often, leaving us in the care of my father. His violent, irrational outbursts increased, and any little thing we did would trigger an eruption. My mother turned a blind eye. We lived in terror of my father's rages. Eventually, I studied karate in high school and learned how to block his blows. He continued to try to hit, punch and kick me, but I was finally able to block every blow while telling him that he could no longer get to me.

The move also meant that my father's sexual acting-out increased dramatically. It was here that he found "the men" and began to engage in ritualized abuse. My father began waking up Erin and me in the middle of the night to bring us to "the basement." We never knew the exact location, but we were taken there by car. We knew it was time to get up and get dressed because my mother would begin singing a particular song. As far as I remember, my mother didn't come with us, but she was party to waking us and getting us out of the house.

Once there, we were joined by other children, all of whom were there to be tortured by a group of men that included my father. There were many psychological techniques used to ensure our compliance. Being tortured and being the "cause" of torture to each other and other children were both punishment for not cooperating. We were given drugs to decrease our fighting back and make it easier for the men to use us to torture others.

When we were in the basement we were not permitted to wear any clothing. Naked, we were forced to crawl from room to room to be tortured, raped and forced to endure experiences designed to induce humiliation, shame and compliance. One of these procedures I came to call "the circle of shame." I was forced to kneel naked in the middle of a circle of men while they spat and urinated on me and called me "whore, slut, cunt, bitch" and other humiliating and degrading names. I choked on the taste of urine in my mouth and my eyes stung when urine penetrated my tightly closed eyelids. I could not dissociate enough to numb myself to the men's laughter as they used me for their sadistic pleasure.

I was gang raped and forced to watch it happen to other children, including my sister. A torturer would hold a gun to my head and play Russian roulette. I was tortured with what I understood to be medical equipment. I was cut, bruised and shocked into submission. There was not an inch of my body that was not violated innumerable times over many years. We returned home like zombies with no memory of the terrible violations we experienced throughout the night.

All this meant that I led two lives: the daytime life and the nighttime life. The conflict and violence between my parents, my father's alcoholism and rages and his physical and sexual abuse were all a part of my daytime life. I have always remembered these events and spoken about them with Erin. The nighttime life in the basement with the ring of men was hidden from my consciousness until I began uncovering the experiences in therapy. While the nighttime activities continued beyond my awareness, my daytime life outside my family flourished. In addition to learning karate, I joined the high school band and chorus. These daytime activities probably saved me from drug and alcohol use and gave me an outlet in school that I desperately needed.

In retrospect, it is clear there were warning signs of my abuse that were ignored. Back in grammar school, despite testing at a genius level, my grades ranged from A's to F's. I also was disruptive in class. Almost every year, my parents were called in to talk with the teacher about my behavior. I don't think they ever took the teachers' concerns seriously or questioned why I was acting out so much. They never did anything to address the teachers' observations to try to help me achieve my full academic potential.

Another ignored sign was that I was in an inordinate number of fights with the boys in the neighborhood. Most of my girlfriends never were in physical fights with the boys in our class, but it was a regular occurrence for me. I knew way too much about physical fighting. Whatever the "reason" for the fight, my parents didn't question why I fought so much.

Even clearer signs of abuse were evident. I was diagnosed with a vaginal infection before the age of 10. The doctor explained to my mother that it was probably because I was wiping my bottom the wrong way. I don't remember the pediatrician asking me anything about someone touching me in inappropriate places. Again, as a sign of the times, no one asked or even thought about abuse in suspect circumstances like this.

Later, in high school, I remember going out with friends to eat a second dinner at McDonald's late in the evening. Now I think it was to have the energy to survive the torture in the middle of the night. I also developed "insomnia," which led to extreme fatigue. I often stayed home to sleep in the mornings and lied about why I was missing classes. Eventually, I was diagnosed with Gilbert's syndrome, a rare, genetically based benign disease that causes extreme fatigue and has no cure. The doctor explained that the only thing that helped was to get as much rest as possible and to take B vitamins. I was shocked when a classmate of mine told me that she also had been diagnosed with Gilbert's syndrome and was going to the same doctor. I didn't realize the significance of this until years later when I remembered having seen this girl in the basement. The doctor was part of the ring of men and used this diagnosis as a convenient explanation for severe sleep deprivation.

My friendships suffered also. I not only blocked the memories of the ritual abuse from myself, I kept the sexual and physical abuse at home hidden from my friends. There was no way for them to understand the shift from a funny, caring and smart person at one moment to a disruptive and out-of-control person the next. I was a leader at times and at other times very disrespectful of those around me.

My sister tells me that I was suicidal on occasion and engaged her and a friend to keep watch. I have no memory of this.

There were some things that helped me survive. I worked at a residential Girl Scout camp for most of the summers during high school. That camp provided the safe haven I needed in nature, campfires, kids and friendships with women who were gentle and fun. I experienced a deep depression when summer was over and it was time to return home for the year. At the time I didn't realize that I was also going back to the nightly torture.

There is one more piece to my history that is important because it was one of the prime reasons I survived psychologically. When I was eight years old, I began taking guitar lessons, which opened the door to playing and singing at Girl Scout camp, church functions and coffee houses. Most important, it was a source of pleasure, a means of escape and a way to find solace for me at home. I regularly closed my bedroom door and retreated to the comfort that playing the guitar offered.

As I finish this brief outline of my early experiences, I am reminded of my mother's refrain to me every time I tried to tell her as an adult how devastating these childhood experiences were for me. Her response has always been, "Don't you remember the good things that happened when you were growing up? It wasn't all bad." No, Mother. It wasn't all bad. I had friends and experiences that sheltered me and helped me avoid developing more severe psychiatric problems. You taught me that a woman could do anything a man can do – still a new concept in the 60s and 70s. When my girlfriends were being primed to become nuns, you supported my dream to be a doctor. You taught me to have a sense of humor and adventure.

My father taught me how to throw a football and play sports. He honed my logic skills through my many arguments with him. My mother gave me the pathway to a strong faith and an open mind to all people. I wish all these gifts were enough to erase the damage done by the years of abuse, torture and neglect. I wish these gifts would enable me to have a strong relationship with my parents as they enter their twilight years. Instead, I have an automatic response of "deer in the headlights" any time I talk to them, or very rarely, see them. That response of terror is encoded in my cells along with my sense of being a strong woman. I will take these memories and their effects with me to my grave.

SUE'S HISTORY

I come to this profession honestly: I grew up in the role of oldest sib and oldest cousin in a relatively "normal" family that was rooted in Christian and humanitarian values. That role led me to become a caretaker who was always interested in what made people tick. Being a therapist also fits my personality: I have always loathed the polite chit-chat of a cocktail party and have found the depth of relationship that can be achieved in the one-on-one therapeutic relationship especially rewarding. I continue to find working as a therapist fascinating, and constantly marvel at the ingenuity, strength, resilience and creativity of my clients. I love learning and find that I am truly learning all the time in my role as therapist.

CHAPTER 1

Before I speak about my professional background as a therapist, I need to refer to my first profession, since it became a key part of my work with Elizabeth. My first degree is in Performance Piano. Although I do not perform as a pianist anymore, I have never really left music. In my family of origin, in my family today and in my free time, music has played a central role. Having left the organized church many years ago, I have relied on music to be my spiritual core. It will become clear later in the book how this part of me was almost as important as all the theoretical discussions that follow.

Not long after college, I went back to school to become a clinical social worker. One of my first clients introduced herself to me as a high-functioning young student, doing well academically, but also reported nonchalantly that she often slept under a tree near her apartment "because it was safe." The disconnect between this bright woman's intellect and her highly risky ways of coping with the traumatic memories that were haunting her was immediately fascinating. This client taught me to understand symptoms as adaptations to the "reality" of traumatic history and to avoid the discounting label of "psychotic behaviors." As we worked together, I also began to understand the "push-pull" so often used to describe the relationship with clients who have suffered traumatic relational experiences. I could see the tremendous human need to connect to another struggling against her considerable and logical fear that any connection had the risk of leading to another trauma. Learning to be empathic with that core dilemma and then walking the line with a client trying to battle those opposing and powerful needs is constantly both fascinating and challenging. The patience required by the therapist is dwarfed by the courage required by the client in this kind of therapeutic relationship. I was intrigued.

Since this is not a book about theory, I will not talk about my ongoing journey through a variety of clinical orientations. A reader familiar with these clinical theories will see and understand their connection to the therapy experience we are describing together. In the final chapter, we will talk about a few over-arching principles that formed the foundation of my thinking and are in accordance with Elizabeth's beliefs as well.

CHAPTER 2

PROCESS

HAVING MADE THE decision to try to write this book, we had to create a framework that would support the complexities of the change in our relationship. To move from 12 years as client and therapist to an entirely different relationship would require a good deal of thoughtful preparation, and we spent two months while still in our roles of therapist and client carefully defining what this new relationship could and couldn't be.

Keenly aware of our shared concerns about the project, we decided on some clear rules:

First, we were to begin as co-writers only, and our relationship would be limited to that. Elizabeth had to commit to not using our new relationship as a place to continue to act as a client, and Sue had to let go of the anonymity of her role as therapist, trusting that the natural process of becoming colleagues would guide her in any decision to share parts of her personal life story. We understood that we were not embarking on a friendship and that there would be no artificial "catch up." We were clear that no further movement toward a different kind of relationship would happen unless we talked about it and were mutually ready.

Second, we had to acknowledge that our book project might not work, so we gave ourselves permission, in that case, to change our minds and give up the process. It was not a decision to write a book, therefore, but simply a decision to try to write together.

Finally, we promised each other to be honest about our experience as we went along and to continually assess how we felt. We both knew how potentially uncomfortable the work would be as we examined eight years of trauma work and looked closely at times that had been difficult for both of us. We gave each other permission to veto a discussion that was too painful. We were also clear that we would disagree and that it would have to be ok to do so. We would edit and challenge each other's writing, definitely a new element in our relationship. We knew that our disagreements, differing perceptions and constant challenges to each other would keep us from easy answers and force us to tease out what actually happened between us.

After 12 years as client and therapist, we both knew intuitively that we could work through just about anything, which made our decision to work together possible, and by the end of our preliminary discussions, we had both become comfortable enough to leave our client/therapist roles. When Elizabeth walked out of Sue's office for the last time, we entered an entirely new relationship with new rules, new expectations, some anxieties and lots of hope that we could make a successful transition.

Evolving as co-authors

We marked the change to our new roles by using Elizabeth's office for our weekly 1½- to 2½-hour meetings. When we began to talk about our therapy experience as clinicians and equal partners, our task looked daunting! We began our first conversations looking at the parts of our therapy that were most confusing to both of us in an effort to begin to understand what had ultimately made our therapy together successful. We were both surprised at how much we were already learning from each other and just how different our individual perspectives and memories of our interactions often were. We knew it was important to look at these individual incidents of misunderstanding but needed some structure to organize our discussions.

After a few weeks, we decided to offer each other a list of questions, with the agreement that we could decline to answer any question if it felt too personal or painful. Our goals were to stimulate our thinking about our therapy and to begin the search for the organizing principles of our book. Out of these conversations came more and more questions, along with feedback to each other about both the confusing moments and the especially powerful ones. We knew there was a lot to write about but still needed a structure. We challenged each other to identify four over-arching factors that would help explain what we were beginning to understand from our conversations. We came back the following week with our lists and discovered enough similarity in our understanding to begin the book under the umbrella of those four factors.

THE FOUR FACTORS

1. Temporary Is Permanent

A lot of our earliest conversations focused on the issue that had topped each of our original lists of questions when we began to work as colleagues: Why had Sue's vacations caused so much turmoil for Elizabeth? It was clear to us that Sue's vacations challenged Elizabeth's ability to sustain her emotional connection to Sue. Even from week to week, Elizabeth struggled to feel connected to Sue, to remember what had happened in session and even to believe that Sue would still be there for the next session. The relationship often felt like we were rebuilding or at least shoring it up every time we met. This dilemma of a tentative sense of connection we called Temporary Is Permanent.

2. Suicide Is Always an Option

We both knew that the continued prevalence of suicidal thinking was of prime importance. A large piece of our therapy dealt with the intense shame Elizabeth felt in having strong suicidal thoughts and feelings, and Sue struggled to avoid discussions of medication and hospitalization that might intensify that shame. Thus, Suicide Is Always an Option became our second factor.

3. The Shame Filter

The difficulty in staying connected with each other and the total missteps that occurred were the hardest to understand and label. We became aware of our very different understandings of certain incidents and conversations. What Sue remembered feeling toward Elizabeth was nothing like what Elizabeth remembered having experienced. Elizabeth was often convinced of Sue's negative beliefs about her that had no basis in Sue's reality. Although the idea of shame as a central experience in working with traumatic material is a well understood phenomenon, the power of Elizabeth's experience of her own shame to distort what was in front of her was more potent than we realized at the time. Over time, the idea of the Shame Filter emerged to explain the phenomenon of two people trying very hard to stay connected in a healing relationship, who were both struggling to be understood, yet were often not being understood at all.

4. Safety Versus Trust

As we began to examine the crucial parts of our relationship, the topic of Safety Versus Trust arose. Though these are not new concepts in working with traumatic material in therapy, we found the need to underline the difference between the two to accurately portray just how risky the process of therapy can be, even when the relationship itself has established itself as trustworthy. It took some time to define the differences between the two concepts, but we felt that the distinction helps explain some of the struggles in our relationship.

DECIDING THE BOOK'S FORMAT

We briefly considered other factors, but ultimately decided that most of our experience could be understood using these four. Once the four factors had been decided, we began focusing on each one and exploring our experiences in their context. Neither of us was focused on theoretical understanding of what was happening, but, rather, we were interested in finding ways of describing our experience together so that other clients and therapists could benefit from our experience. Both of us naturally kept bringing in examples from our work together to illustrate further our exploration. It seemed logical to use these examples, which we call "vignettes," to illustrate our very specific experiences through the lens of the four factors. Elizabeth had kept diaries during our therapy and Sue had extensive notes. We could look back at this raw material for the vignettes to illustrate our different experiences and show what had worked and what had not. Just as with the understanding we had during our earliest conversations, we gave each other permission to veto any vignette that was too painful, but we also understood that the more open and honest we could be, the better the picture of our therapy would be. We worked hard to avoid deleting important stories and to talk through anything that seemed initially embarrassing or difficult to see in print. In the end, there were very few vetoes, and we feel we are telling our story with as much accuracy and honesty as our memories permit.

We did not want to sanitize in any way the nature of what our therapy had been like, hoping to recapture the feelings at the moment as best we could. We have avoided giving specific details of Elizabeth's abuse to steer clear of any sensationalism and stay focused on the therapy relationship. In the vignettes, even when confusion later gave way to understanding, we tried to illustrate the confusion first, before the eventual resolution. Because we tried to avoid whitewashing the messy parts, our therapy does not read like a smoothly orchestrated step-by-step process. There are very few "Eureka!" moments of sudden understanding so often seen in textbooks.

We wrote as we went along and eventually started meeting every other week when writing took more and more time. We consistently checked in with each other about how we were feeling and discussed our changing relationship as we went along. We let the casual sharing of small parts of our personal lives unfold naturally.

There were bumps and misunderstandings and times when we both wondered if our process would work. We had to allow ourselves to be frustrated with each other at times and had to work at being open about our level of comfort and commitment as the writing process went on. At times the project was idle for months because of personal schedules and illnesses.

Despite all that, a wonderful thing happened from all this attention to our relationship and our careful preparation for being co-writers: We arrived at a new place as colleagues and collaborators. We found mutual fascination in our close examination of our therapy together and excitement in sorting our experience in a coherent way. We wanted to tell our story.

CHAPTER 3

FINDING THE RIGHT WORDS

Beginning therapy

THE FOCUS OF this book is on a therapy that involved new traumatic memories and the aftermath of that therapeutic work. However, there was a significant amount of work done before those memories surfaced that lay the foundation for the work on new traumatic memories that followed. Elizabeth came into therapy with the presenting problem of generalized anxiety from multiple stressors, especially her grief around her relationship with her parents, from whom she had been estranged for five years. She also identified career decisions and eating issues as other areas of focus. Elizabeth shared the stories of her abuse that she had always known during this period and focused on grieving the loss of most of her connections with her family of origin and on coping with what she already knew.

We found that our relationship changed a great deal when, after four years of therapy together, Elizabeth began having new memories of traumatic experiences. We have termed this second part of our relationship as "trauma time," differentiating it from our earlier work together, or "pre-trauma time."

It may be useful to describe that pre-trauma time, because that period, unbeknownst to either of us, laid the foundation for the trauma work to come.

Pre-trauma time
Sue's first impressions
When Elizabeth entered therapy, she impressed me immediately with her warmth and intelligence and the clarity of her goals for therapy. She had had a very positive experience with her prior therapist and seemed to me to feel fairly comfortable in the client role. Elizabeth entered therapy having done some work earlier on memories involving physical, sexual and

psychological abuse from an alcoholic father, and neither of us anticipated a therapy that would be uncovering new material. Elizabeth's life at the time was stable, her relationships were solid and our therapy had an ebb and flow with lots of inherent ease. Our interactions were comfortable, and we slowly came to recognize some strong connections between us. As clinicians in the same city, we saw each other at conferences, espousing similar views. We discovered each other to be feminists and people interested in social justice. It became clear that we shared similar values, politics and ways of being in the world. We still kept within the normal therapist/client roles, but during our non-trauma time relationship, we came to know each other enough to feel a shared sense of identity. We both knew that had we met outside of the therapist/client role, we would have been friends.

I think it is important to note here that although the vignettes in Elizabeth's voice focus almost exclusively on her experience as someone in the midst of trauma and all its complexities, she was also struggling to continue a normal life. Remarkably, she was working and engaged with her partner and a wide circle of friends. She occasionally led workshops, cared for sick friends and eventually took various music lessons. There were many times when maintaining that normal life was extremely difficult, but she never quit her work, nor dropped out of her life in any other significant way.

Elizabeth's first impressions

My first impression of Sue was in our initial phone conversation. I had asked her about how she would feel working with a lesbian client. Although I don't remember her exact words, she responded as if it was a non-issue, and it was clear that she would be accepting. Once meeting her face to face, I felt she could accept me without pathologizing. Very quickly into our time together the family issues I initially brought in faded away and work and eating issues took center stage. Sue was open, nonjudgmental and easy to talk with. She was eager to understand me and to know what I needed from her. I felt she was trustworthy. We quickly saw that we shared similar values and understanding about the therapy process.

Trauma time and the "muck"

Before we can begin to illustrate what trauma time was like for us by describing our four main factors, we must start with what we have called "the muck." We have searched for a more formal word, but have not found one that describes the experience of being in the middle of an intense relationship, full of horrific memories, that is complicated by the four factors that we ultimately have delineated. The muck is the experience we had while in the middle of trauma work, before we had much language at all to describe what it felt like to each of us. It was the collision of four years of therapy history with an onslaught of trauma memories that rendered that history largely meaningless. It was the confusion of words exchanged whose meanings were suddenly challenged or misunderstood in profound ways. It was sailing in uncharted waters with a partner who suddenly became untrustworthy after years of mutual trust. It was meeting someone you believed you knew and suddenly discovering parts of her you had never seen. It was living with the potential for suicide on a daily basis.

Muck seems a perfect image because it is the opposite of clarity. You can't see much in the muck. You can slog through it, but it is slow going, and you don't exactly know where the ground is. To keep the image going a bit longer, it also stays with you; it's hard to leave behind. For us, that meant that after a session, we each asked ourselves what had happened. It often meant that an understanding of our verbal exchange wasn't reached for days and sometimes even weeks. Because nothing was the way either of us wanted, our frustration and the exhaustion of getting through the muck meant anger directed at each other. It meant an ongoing experience of exhaustion. There was rarely a moment that we could just take that "walk in the park" for a change. We looked for other paths and longed for a break. These were times when the subject of medication or hospitalization briefly surfaced. We both wrote, in journals and client notes, as a way of trying to make some sense of what was happening.

During therapy while in the midst of this muck, we struggled to understand our experience, knowing that tending our relationship was key. That often meant sharing our experience of the relationship in the moment, even when that relationship felt pretty shaky at best. Sometimes deep theoretical discussions took place as a way of trying to organize and understand what was not working. Sometimes intuitive decisions were made that significantly shifted the dynamics of the moment and helped us get out of them. The nonverbal activities we describe later fall into this category.

Sometimes we were able to empathically share with each other our separate, but similar, frustrations, disappointments and exhaustion, providing a connection in the midst of the muck, even while there was still little clarity. Sometimes Elizabeth would be able to write after the fact and help Sue understand what had happened to her in a session. Sometimes Sue was able to understand her own "stuck places" after the fact and share that with Elizabeth. Because each of us was experienced in trauma work, we could sometimes fall back on our clinical understandings for some comfort it the midst of the chaos. It helped to be reminded that some of this was normal. We both kept trying, and we both were committed, even if the motivations for that commitment were different. We both knew that "dry land and clear views" were a long walk away.

As we wrote our book, it was the memory of the muck that gave us the urgency to talk for hours about it to gain clarity for ourselves, and, as a result, we came to a far deeper understanding of what our experience was. The four factors we formulated have given us ready language to talk about our experiences and to sort them out with greater understanding. We hope that these factors will allow readers to understand what contributed to the muck and help them understand why therapy that focuses on trauma can be so complicated. However, we do not want to imply that the clarity of hindsight was part of our experience in the moment. There were times, of course, when we could clearly see where we were getting stuck and work through that experience. There were times when one of us had some ideas about what was going on. There were times when understanding of the muck came eventually. But most of the time, the four factors overlapped, interacted and intensified each other to create the muck we trudged through in the heat of trauma time.

Each of the following chapters describes one factor and how it affected our therapy experience. We have used vignettes in the personal voice of each of us, taken from our notes and journals, to illustrate our separate perspectives and to show how different our views were at times. We hope that the vignettes, chosen as model moments that illustrate each factor, will show the complexity of our process as well as some of the ways we dealt with each factor. We hope they give an idea of the confusion, pain and work that we did that led to misses and misunderstandings as well as successful moments.

CHAPTER 4

TEMPORARY IS PERMANENT

OUR FIRST FACTOR addresses the major challenges we found to using our relationship as a major "tool" in our therapy. As a reminder to the reader, we are not discounting other tried-and-true techniques or ways of understanding the process of therapy involving trauma. We are stating that in this particular story, the relationship was our best and necessary focus. We recognize that we are far from alone in this understanding.

Practically every text, lecture or discussion of therapy of any kind refers to the primacy of "the relationship," though just what that means is often left to the imagination. There are specific characteristics that define the relationship between therapist and client, such as the shared goals, the roles and limitations of both therapist and client, time parameters, confidentiality, who is sharing what, etc. There are also many qualities of the therapy relationship that are the same as in any relationship. If we are to emphasize the importance of a "genuine" relationship, we first need to define what that can look like. It is some of these normal expectations of relationships that need to be articulated to understand what we experienced in our trauma work when these expectations became unreliable or completely unfounded. Since we consider genuineness and authenticity as an important part of the therapeutic relationship, it might be safe to assume that there was an "authentic" relationship between us that would look like many other relationships outside the therapy office.

It is these assumptions that were consistently challenged and sometimes shattered by our first main theme, Temporary Is Permanent. We define Temporary Is Permanent as *a dynamic in trauma time in which the client does not feel any predictability or certainty about her relationship with her therapist, despite the amount of history between them. Normal assumptions about a shared relationship are not reliable.*

First, it should be noted that in Elizabeth's pre-trauma time, the dilemma of Temporary Is Permanent was not seen, and the more normal assumptions about relationships were in play. Elizabeth experienced Sue as reliable and empathic. Sue saw Elizabeth as engaged and self-reliant. We had a history of working hard together, laughing and trusting that our relationship was pretty solid. There had been changes in our schedule, including a six-month period when Elizabeth stopped therapy. There were vacations, conferences and illness that interrupted our time together. There were misunderstandings and missteps, as well. None of these, however, ever threatened our relationship in any serious way. Our relationship seemed fairly reliable to both of us, and that made for relatively smooth sailing. We assumed then that we would be able to weather any storm, and re-group after any interruption.

It was when trauma time arrived that the familiarity and predictability of our relationship disappeared and we lost that foundation. With the onset of traumatic memories, assumptions that we had both made about our relationship were no longer valid and everything was up for questioning. There was no "built" relationship, no shared understanding and no reliable memory of our history together. A shaky sense of trust and levels of intimacy that ricocheted from close to impossibly distant replaced it.

It also should be noted that we are aware there were other issues that contributed to the relationship feeling unstable. We are talking about trauma that occurred in the context of a relationship with someone who was well known, so any therapy that counts on the relationship being part of a healing process is in tricky waters. Even a temporary feeling of connection, safety or intimacy in the therapy relationship can feel simultaneously positive and very risky for anyone who has been abused in a relationship. There was a reality for Elizabeth that even sought-after connection could increase her feelings of danger and cause her to look for ways to distance herself from Sue, the perceived source of that danger.

We will first look at these "normal assumptions" about relationships that we found unreliable in trauma time due to Temporary Is Permanent.

Assumption 1: "Relationships are built"

The first major assumption that proved unreliable was that relationships are built between people over time. Gradually, two people increasingly "know" each other and their relationship builds on its own history. For example, the therapist/client relationship of five years clearly feels different from the first session — even if we enter the office with clarity about being in the moment and making no assumptions with the client – new or well known. Each person enters with some idea of what to expect, given the length and breadth of the history of that particular relationship, even while being available to new experiences that will build on prior experiences. In a relationship between friends, for example, you know whom to call to see a particular movie, because you "know" and anticipate that she will like it. In therapy, it may be a therapist who gives out information about an upcoming vacation with some expectation that the client will react in similar ways to prior vacation notification. For a client, it may mean trusting that therapist will be able to hear an increasingly difficult memory, since a prior memory was well received.

For us, once trauma time began, Elizabeth could no longer believe what she had known about Sue. There was no building on our history, and in fact, history was not available. It didn't matter that we had already been seeing each other in therapy for several years; it was just no longer possible to assume Sue's patterns, expectations or personality traits or believe in the reliability of our relationship. With nothing available as permanent, Elizabeth was left in a constant state of uncertainty and fear. As a result, she was distrustful and on guard with Sue, despite a history that had been built on trust, caring and respect.

Assumption 2: "Participants in a relationship have a shared understanding of their experience of the relationship"

Another assumption is that there is a shared understanding and even though each person will have her own unique perspective, the two views will align enough to not disrupt the connection. This means that the therapist and client would have similar understandings of what happened in a session, similar explanations for misunderstandings and similar assessments of the therapy process itself. We do not mean to imply that their views would be identical, but that if they were to describe the session to each other, they would generally agree to what happened, even if they had slightly different takes on it, had slightly different meanings or different parts of the session had more meaning for either the client or therapist.

In trauma time, the new reality meant that we did not have this shared understanding of our relationship. Part of the difficulty in talking with each other about what was happening between us was that we suddenly did not view our relationship in the same way. Sue could no longer trust the assumptions of how things would work out between us because Elizabeth was suddenly without reference points. In a very disconcerting way, it felt like we were in a brand new relationship, with largely unknown rules.

Because of the loss of a shared understanding, we also no longer had a "shared history," since Elizabeth did not have consistent access to memories of who Sue was or how she had acted over the years. Despite understanding some of the difficulties Elizabeth was having, Sue was remembering the prior sessions and continuing to hold in her mind the history of the relationship. Elizabeth could not count on having that capacity. It often became important for Sue to help Elizabeth reconstruct a session or conversation in order to not misunderstand Sue's intentions. It was confusing for Sue to continually need to repeat herself, reassure Elizabeth of what had been completely understood before and to realize that the only exchange between them that really counted was the one they were having at that particular moment. There was to be no relying on our shared past, since it was at best only inconsistently available to Elizabeth.

It's important to clarify that we are not referring to the loss of memory. Certainly, that can happen in therapy when a client is in the midst of healing from trauma, but that is not what we are talking about here. In our case, Elizabeth sometimes forgot what had been said in session. However, the complexity of Temporary Is Permanent meant that Elizabeth often could "remember" the words said, but sometimes was not able to have a sense that she could believe what she remembered or use it in any way to help herself in the moment. Without access to the context of our shared understanding of our history, those words held little sway. Sue continued to show empathy and support, but there was no way for Elizabeth to hold on to that, given that the history of her words and their reliability were not available at all. Elizabeth was left with only the experience in the moment on which to form her reality. With the demons of trauma nearby and all the chaos around, an extremely fragile and easily changeable experience was all that was possible for us.

It is also important to note that we are not talking about the dissociative experience (*an experience of feeling detached from feelings or even from the body in which the reality is challenged and memory is unreliable*), even though there were times when Elizabeth was dissociative. We found that Temporary Is Permanent was a sort of constant state of mind, induced by being in the middle of horrific memories, that kept Elizabeth from being able to remember and trust our history. Neither are we talking about "being in a flashback" (*having an acute experience of reliving a traumatic event*), even though, again, there were isolated times when that was the case. Temporary Is Permanent was a pervasive and powerful ongoing experience. While conversations between us looked no different on the "outside" than they had before we entered trauma time, the experience each of us had of that conversation was significantly changed.

Assumption 3: "Memory of the other in the relationship is reliable"

A third assumption is that in the absence of the other, there is a reasonably reliable picture of that person; i.e., we can recall her, remember the level of connection and find reassurance in knowing that she remains constant even in absence. As friends, for example, we might know that our college roommate would welcome a call out of nowhere and we can "pick right up from where we left off"— a sure sign of a good relationship. For a client, it might mean that during a two-week absence from therapy, the client may miss seeing her therapist, but is confident that she will return and that they too can "pick right up from where we left off."

For us, Elizabeth's erratic ability to recall the relationship between us meant that each session felt in some ways like a brand new exchange. Elizabeth could not always reference our history to reassure herself of Sue's good intentions, trust that Sue would be empathic and not judgmental or allow for a misstep to mean less than a sure-fire indication that she could not be trusted.

Assumption 4: "Relationships have a shared experience of the level of safety"

We also assume that as the relationship continues, there is a parallel growth in a shared sense of reliability, trust and safety, even if the amount of trust or safety varies from person to person. In many ways, this assumption is dependent on the first three. Safety in the relationship is built over time and requires both a comfortable level of understanding and a shared history that can support a feeling of safety. For example, as good friends we may ask each other for a favor – a risk we wouldn't take if we didn't have some sense that it would be granted. As a therapist, we might invite a deeper question into the room, knowing that there was some sense of comfort established. As a client, it might mean risking sharing a difficult story or exposing a shameful experience, believing that the history between the client and therapist reassured the client that it would be safe enough to do so.

In trauma time, we no longer shared a reliable sense of safety in our relationship. Although we devote a full chapter to this topic because if its complexity, it's important to note that there was a loss of this assumption between us as we moved from pre-trauma time to trauma time. All of the assumptions about relationships that we have been discussing contribute to an overall experience of safety in a relationship. Not being able to recall the comfort that the safety between us had offered was both a shock and disappointment, shaking a core part of what we both thought had been there. Given that traumatic memories abound with experiences of the lack of safety, the loss of that safety was profound to us.

Assumption 5: *"Relationships exist on some continuum of intimacy"*

The result of all these elements is that the relationship between two people has some level of intimacy that usually deepens with time, if well tended. Certainly, the friendship of 20 years is experienced differently than that of a few weeks. In therapy, although the length of time may not reach that extreme, the intensity of the relationship often compresses that process, allowing for a level of intimacy that is not as frequent in friendships. As time goes on in a therapeutic relationship, there is a deeper understanding between the therapist and client. As friends, history, reliability and safety form the foundation of an increased level of intimacy. Although there are no guarantees, of course, the potential is there for a growth in connection.

For us, we vacillated between experiences of intimacy and times when we felt virtually no connection at all. There were moments of intimacy around sharing of difficult memories or repairing our relationship, followed by moments of such a level of misunderstanding and disconnection that we may well have been strangers. Thus, there was no "progression" of intimacy.

Temporary Is Permanent challenged all the assumptions about relationships mentioned above and rendered them unreliable. We hope to show in the following vignettes what Temporary Is Permanent looked like and how we battled it, whether on the "mega-level" of vacations or in the moment-to-moment exchanges. It is clear only in retrospect how powerful this factor was in determining the experience of our relationship.

The impact of Temporary Is Permanent on any misunderstanding that occurred was enormous. In our non-trauma time relationship, if Sue unintentionally hurt Elizabeth, we could use the trust we had in our history to combat the impact and put it in some historical context. With discussion and with referencing that relationship and its reliability and safety, we could sort it out, repair whatever was needed, and the relationship could continue relatively undamaged. In fact, the relationship between us often was experienced as strengthened by the process of working through the misunderstanding. With Temporary Is Permanent, there were no such tools available and very few ways to combat the power of the experience when Temporary Is Permanent was in full force. The following vignettes will illustrate this struggle as well as show some of the ways we tried to battle Temporary Is Permanent.

TEMPORARY IS PERMANENT FIRST SHOWS ITSELF

The most emblematic experience we shared that highlighted the Temporary Is Permanent factor was when a break in our appointment schedule occurred. It was difficult enough for Elizabeth to have some sense of our relationship when we were actually together, but with Sue's absence, Elizabeth's ability to hold onto the relationship was severely challenged. This first vignette focuses on the impact a necessitated change in availability had on our newly fragile connection. Because suicidal thoughts and feelings arrived with great intensity with the new memories, we had almost daily contact for the first several months. A shift in Sue's schedule occurred very early in the trauma time when the chaos was new and Elizabeth's responses out of Temporary Is Permanent were surprising in their intensity. None of her intellectual understanding of how reasonable Sue's regular vacation was could diminish the terror of abandonment that had been rekindled by new traumatic memories. The next vignettes illustrate our very different sense of the moment.

Elizabeth: Cutting back on contact time

I was furious with Sue. On the phone over the weekend she made it very clear that she no longer had the time to talk with me as much as she had been. When I saw her today, I brought up the phone conversation and told her my feelings about what she'd said. Sue said that she'd told me this before now — I didn't believe her. Maybe she'd hinted that her schedule was changing, but she never said what this would mean for our contact. I told her on the phone this weekend that I noticed how she wasn't as available as she used to be. I thought it meant that she was tired of me and finally figured out that I just wasn't worth all of the time that she'd been spending with me.

Sue explained that she originally thought that when the first memory surfaced, I had entered a state of emotional emergency that would settle down in a few weeks. She hadn't anticipated that it would continue or that new memories would surface. Sue also explained that now her schedule wasn't as flexible as it had been over the past two months. With her teaching schedule beginning again she wouldn't be able to spend as much time with me.

I was ashamed to admit that I was devastated by this news. I was terrified of not being able to talk to Sue when my emotions seemed out of my control. What would I do if the suicidal thinking became too overwhelming and I couldn't reach her? I felt ashamed to tell anyone else how much I thought of suicide. What if I had another memory and I became so paralyzed I couldn't leave the house to go to work? I couldn't call clients and tell them that I was too traumatized to see them today. What if I couldn't sleep for days because of the daily nightmares? I already had such bad insomnia that I was lucky to get four hours of sleep at night. What if the insomnia got worse because memories and emotions dammed up from not being able to talk to Sue almost every day? I knew I was panicking, and I felt like a loser for having these feelings. I would have been lying to myself, though, if I denied them. I was on the verge of losing my mind and had no one to trust. Sue wouldn't be here for me anymore. I was on my own again.

I knew that once Sue realized what a loser I was, she would cut back on the time she spent with me. And I was right. Sue swore that it wasn't the case. Ha, how was I supposed to believe her? And even if I did, it didn't make me less vulnerable. Those flashbacks still haunted me. My nightmares and insomnia were worse than ever. I was doomed.

Sue: Talk about a mistake!

Today I reminded Elizabeth that, as I had told her earlier, I would need to find a new, more-limited time schedule to see her. I explained that with summer over, my client load had increased and I was again teaching, leaving me with far fewer available hours. I suggested twice a week, each a double session, with phone calls between as needed. I admit to having had some concerns about this discussion because I knew it would be difficult for her, but I was shocked at her response. First of all, I had warned her several times earlier, but she seemed not to remember. Second, the level of pain was off the charts. I was watching her experience abandonment at my hands. Not a great feeling.

I also was thrown by the confusion of our completely different perspectives. I was referencing the four-year history we had together and was assuming that Elizabeth was able to do that, as well. I was shocked as I began to realize that we might as well have just met. She could not believe that my changed availability meant anything other that a statement of abandonment. I found myself scrambling to reassure her that it was not the case, but it felt like I was up against a wall that would not easily be broached. She left the session feeling devastated by me and nothing I said seemed to have made any impact.

Elizabeth: The first vacation during trauma time

Sue told me today that she was going on vacation again. I totally fell apart. I shut down and couldn't think at all. I went into a total panic. I didn't understand myself. I'd been seeing Sue for years now and she had consistently gone on several vacations a year at around the same time. Until now when Sue would tell me that she was going on vacation, I usually would think about the money I would save. Sometimes I wished that she weren't going away because the timing was bad for me, but I never panicked or felt abandoned by her. This morning was different. I thought I would never see her again. I thought it meant she hated me and was running away from me. I tried to stop thinking that but I couldn't. I sat withdrawn and silent in Sue's office. I couldn't explain what was happening – I couldn't form the words.

I hated myself for how I felt. It was just a goddamned vacation, but I felt so abandoned. When we talked almost every day, I didn't have to worry if Sue would disappear. I knew no one should have to talk to me while she was on vacation – let alone every day. I had never needed to talk to Sue while she was on vacation before all of this damned trauma shit started. But now I was a total basket case.

At the end of our session, Sue said she would call me during her vacation at our regularly scheduled appointment times. We also set up a time to talk on the phone the first day of her vacation. Sue had seen how much I was struggling, and I was grateful for her generosity. I wasn't sure I could have gone back to see her after her vacation if she hadn't offered this. I would have felt too betrayed.

TEMPORARY IS PERMANENT IN MOMENT-TO-MOMENT INTERACTIONS

Temporary Is Permanent went far beyond the vacation dilemma. From session to session, or even within a session, this dynamic was ever present. It was one of the factors that led to that muck feeling of confusion, frustration and swirling emotions that were always changing. Both of us were trying, caring and working hard, but were constantly being tripped up by the chaos of trauma time with Temporary Is Permanent right in the middle of it. Sue kept unconsciously reverting to assumptions that Elizabeth would remember their history and be able to apply it as we went along. That would mean, for example, that if she reassured Elizabeth she could call anytime, the offer was still on the table, even if Sue didn't recommit to this during every session. We discovered, however, that was not the case. There were many times within a session or between sessions when Sue made these kinds of assumptions only to find that Elizabeth was not able to operate with the same assumptions. Consequently, she thought Elizabeth understood her intentions only to find that she did not. This confusion was a constant companion.

These vignettes illustrate one way we tried to combat Temporary Is Permanent and serve as examples of the confusion Temporary Is Permanent causes with two very different understandings of a session.

Sue: Reporting in
Today Elizabeth asked me to leave her a message after our session,

summarizing what we talked about. We talked quite a bit about this. She told me that she was having a hard time remembering and trusting our sessions, remembering what we talked about and remembering that I cared for her. I was very hesitant to honor her request, for several reasons. I worried that what I pulled out of the session as "important" wouldn't be what was important to her, and that I unwittingly would be valuing parts of our time together and not mentioning others. I worried that my take on the session might preclude hers and subtly discourage her perceptions. While Elizabeth understood my concerns, she was adamant that it would be more helpful than hurtful. She really needed something to help her remember what had transpired during the session and hoped that this would help her do that. I agreed to try it, with the understanding that we would revisit it to see how it was feeling to her.

Elizabeth: Not remembering my request

I couldn't believe what happened with Sue today. I sat down and she immediately started to tell me about a therapy group she had found for me at a local hospital. I couldn't believe it. She was finally throwing me out. She knew how much I worried that she'd leave me. When she told me about this group I thought she was really telling me that this was the end of our relationship — the first step to getting me out of her office for good. I sat through most of the session feeling extremely hurt and furious. Then something even more bizarre happened. Sue asked me if I remembered asking her to find other resources for me. She said that I asked her to look for a group therapy program or something else so that I could get more support. I had absolutely no recollection of asking her this. For a few seconds I thought she was kidding. She wasn't. Apparently, I had asked Sue last week if she could find more resources for me so I wouldn't have to rely on her so much and because I felt I needed more.

Sue was relieved when I told her I had no memory of asking her to find these resources. She said that she had no idea why I was acting the way I was during the session. I was glad she thought to ask or I would have left her office feeling so abandoned that it would have been almost impossible to continue in therapy with her. I knew this was an overreaction, and I felt ashamed. If Sue hadn't asked if I remembered making my request, I would have been totally devastated, and for what?

I knew I was having a hard time holding onto things. I knew I forgot things that happened during sessions. But I didn't think I would forget something that I had to think about before getting to the session. After the session I went home and looked at my journals to see if I had mentioned asking Sue about resources. I discovered that I had written about the session when I asked her to look for a therapy group for me, but I had no memory of actually asking her. This trauma process was frustrating, mind-boggling and sometimes scary. Nothing is permanent. How was I supposed to figure out what and who to trust when I couldn't even trust my own memory?

What was equally terrifying was that I was convinced Sue would do something like this to me. As I wrote about this, I believed Sue would have approached the situation differently if she had indeed initiated the possibility of my using other resources. Well, most of me could believe it. Yet, when she began to talk about this group therapy, I immediately believed that it was the first step to getting rid of me as a client. I had such a hard time remembering the kind of person Sue is. She doesn't throw away people or give up on anyone. But I was a "throw-away person," so it made complete sense to me that Sue had finally thrown me away too. It was hard for me to know how much I could trust her to still care about me when I couldn't use the positive history between us as a touchstone. Right now, everything was shifting. I couldn't keep up, and it made everything so difficult. I felt ashamed and defeated.

Sue: Confusion reigns

Today's session left me completely confused. We began by working on a new memory that Elizabeth had recalled yesterday. It was quite horrific, and took most of the session. My "barometer" read that we were doing OK with it – she was able to continue the story and I was able to stay in an empathic connection to that story – and I was feeling pretty connected with her as we went through it. She seemed to be having a similar experience, and I had no information that anything else was happening. Then, suddenly, she stopped talking and looked sullenly withdrawn. I considered the possibility that she had become nervous that she'd "told" her story and that old dictates from her perpetrators about what would happen if she told had come back to haunt her. I gently tried to inquire about that possibility, but got no response. She had clammed up and just wasn't talking. I asked if there was anything I could do to help her and got stony silence in return. I let some silence go by and tried again to let her know that I wanted to help her if I could. She left the session without saying another word. I must have injured her in some way, but I had to wait to find out what happened. It was as if the first half of the session didn't exist. It was crazy-making! Had I completely misread our connection?

Elizabeth: Soul weary

I had just gotten home from seeing Sue, and I was so soul weary. By battling though continuous struggles and internal censors, I was able to tell Sue the details of the new memory I had the day before. But shortly after finally forming all of the words to describe what happened, I was so overwhelmed with shame that I couldn't say another word for the rest of the session. I tried to talk. I could not. As I sat there, I became more and more angry. I could hear Sue tell me that she was worried, that she wanted to help me if she could. But I couldn't believe her. The overwhelming emotions that accompanied the memory made me feel like I was sitting with a stranger. I had been captured by the feelings of terror and the cruelty of this memory. Sue was in the room with me but "she" didn't really exist. I tried to remind myself that I could trust her. I tried to talk more. I wanted and needed to speak. Instead of opening my mouth, instead of knowing that I was with Sue and that she was safe and had stood by me through so many awful memories, all I could see was a stranger sitting with me who couldn't be trusted. When I could convince myself that Sue wasn't a complete stranger, the overwhelming shame made me feel so covered with slime that I knew that no one, including Sue, could care about me after hearing about this new memory.

I could tell that Sue was confused. Probably frustrated. I stopped talking mid-sentence, didn't say another word and was so angry with myself for not being able to speak that I stormed out of her office.

WHO ARE YOU? WHO AM I?

The impact of the Temporary Is Permanent dilemma was huge. The inability to use our history together in times of disruptions, memory confusion or moments of insecurity made what was already a crisis even bigger. To complicate matters, Elizabeth's struggle was not consistent. There were times when she was far enough removed from her trauma to see Sue as a trusted ally, to know who she was and to use her as a resource. But that was not something either of us could count on. We were forced to travel between a deep knowing and trusting of each other to a completely different stance, where our story had to be written over and over again, as if it never had existed. The process was confusing and exhausting.

The next vignettes show that as this dynamic became clearer to us, we tried to battle directly, sometimes having some success and sometimes not.

Elizabeth: Please use these words

Yesterday I hated my session with Sue. I was feeling so much shame that I could not believe Sue didn't mind being with me and didn't find me disgusting. I told her that. She asked what would help, and after a long silence and battling through a lot of shame, I was able to tell her that I wished that she could say, "Elizabeth, I love you and I'm not leaving you." But she thought I was trying to control her and couldn't understand that only these particular words would sound genuine to me. When Sue didn't immediately say them, I became convinced that she had never really cared about me and that she had been playing the role of the "good therapist" all along. She had to listen and act interested. She had to pretend she cared. But when she couldn't use those words and mean them, I finally knew that she wasn't able to act anymore. I was so screwed. I was in the middle of remembering such horror that I felt I was two seconds away from losing my mind. I couldn't tell anyone else about these experiences and now I found that Sue was only pretending to care. How could I have been so stupid to believe her? I needed to trust her so badly. I felt desperate. I thought I shouldn't go back to see her. She had been mocking me all along, pretending to care and then going on vacation when she knew I felt the most desperate and hopeless. What happened in yesterday's session seemed to confirm all that.

But as I wrote this, I didn't know if it was true. Yesterday I was convinced of it. Why didn't she want to use the words I asked her to use? I would have thought that would make things easier for her. She said she would try, but I don't think she meant it. Sue had told me I was special to her and that she respected my clinical judgments and knowledge. How could I put all of this information together? Not all of her clients were psychologists. She probably had never given a client music books when she went on vacation. If I knew that I was special to her then I could go to the next session and try to talk about what happened between us yesterday. If I could believe that she knew who I was and admired things about me, then I could believe that she actually saw me and not a "generic client." As I wrote this, I believed it. I didn't know if I'd be able to believe it when I saw Sue the next day. So, our next session might let us feel closer again or I could end up knowing what a big mistake I'd made by trusting her at all.

Sue: Finding the "right" words

Today I became really frustrated with Elizabeth. I tried to be patient with her requests, but it felt like I was turning into a robot and that my own capacity for being in the moment had to be turned off. We had a conversation about how awful she felt as a person when she remembered some of what happened to her as a child. She was convinced she was unlovable, disgusting and unworthy of my caring. I tried to speak to that, to tune into her experience and reassure her. However, my words weren't convincing and Elizabeth got angry. She was convinced I was insincere and that I had "always" seen her as unworthy, I was "faking it" and I couldn't wait until she left therapy. She went on to say that I had "never" been able to see her or hear her. There seemed to be no way in. Words that I had said only half an hour ago were forgotten. Finally, she told me the words I could say that would help. I eventually repeated them to her, but I have to admit I felt like a bad actress, reading my lines. They weren't my words, they didn't come from me organically at that moment. I also felt like I was subtly being chastised for not knowing what she needed. It was a no-win experience for both of us. Elizabeth was only somewhat reassured, but I felt inauthentic and shamed. It felt a little crazy-making to me: I thought I had been consistently supportive of her, doing everything I could not to shame her, regularly offering her extra time and yet she seemed to either not remember any of that, or not trust it at all. I began to wonder if I really had been supporting her enough. It ended up feeling like an indictment of my capacity to be with her as well as a disavowal of all that I had said to her for years. It was so hard to realize that Elizabeth couldn't keep that with her, no matter how many times I said the same things.

Sue: Dreading telling Elizabeth about vacation

I make it a policy to tell my clients three weeks before a vacation, so there is plenty of advanced warning. Last Thursday, I should have told Elizabeth about my upcoming summer vacation, but I couldn't bring myself to do it. She had made it clear that if I was going to tell her, I needed to do it at the beginning of the session so she would have time to talk about it with me. When the first few minutes passed by, I slid into the conversation, ignoring the voice in my head that told me to "tell her *now!*"

This morning it was even harder to tell her. The pattern had been repeated many times since the memories started. No matter how much advanced warning, no matter how consistent our contact time had been when I was away, each time was experienced as a new threat to our relationship and to Elizabeth's ability to hang on to any sense that I cared for her. I dreaded it. I ended up feeling like a perpetrator of unspeakable acts. I was rendered unable to offer any comfort – a pretty big loss for someone who considers that part of the job. She became inconsolable, and I ended up feeling ashamed of myself for even considering a vacation, despite all the rational parts of me that were quite comfortable with my schedule.

Sure enough, this morning was a repeat. Elizabeth went into a deep panic when I told her and was clearly frightened at the prospect of two weeks without face-to-face contact. She asked for reassurance that I cared about her, that I would return, that she could still call me and that I wouldn't forget her. It was easy to give her that, though my sense was that it was only of minimal help. It was sad that I couldn't convince her of any of that and reminding her of past vacations was of so little help.

Elizabeth: It doesn't matter who leaves

I was attending a professional conference and would be there for almost a week. More importantly, I would miss two sessions with Sue. I was really panicked about this. For once, it was my leaving rather than Sue's travel plans that necessitated our missing sessions. I had hoped I wouldn't feel so panicked. That was not the case. I was just as terrified of going to this conference as I was when Sue told me that she was going on another vacation. I thought about not attending the conference so I wouldn't have to miss two sessions. But I had traveled to the conference with Jill and I didn't think she would have been very happy if I canceled at the last minute because I couldn't leave my therapist. That sounded so sick. I'd been looking forward to this conference. So, not to be in a panic mode throughout my time here, I set up phone sessions with Sue. Thankfully, she was open to doing that. I felt like an idiot for having to plan this but I really had to. When Sue and I weren't physically together, I often believed that I ceased to exist for her. I didn't feel a closeness or bond with her after I'd left her office. I wasn't sure how present I'd be while I was at the conference. I'd been asking myself, "Will memories flood me and rob me of whatever is happening in the present? Will I ever be able to find Sue again? Will she remember me when I call her?

Will she let me call her? Will she take this opportunity to get rid of me? Will she tell me that she no longer wants to be my therapist?"

As it turned out, I didn't have to worry about Sue forgetting me. I had just gotten off the phone with her. We had a "regular" session. I had to leave the conference and go back to my room to talk with her. I was missing some important interactions at the conference but I absolutely had to talk to Sue. Without this contact she didn't exist for me. That meant I was alone with all of the terrible memories and the terror until we could have contact. Talking on the phone wasn't as reassuring as actually seeing her, but I was reassured that I could still count on her. She'd seen me through so much. I wasn't sure how she put up with me. When I asked her that today, she said she was in this for the long haul. She explained that she "knew what she signed up for" and was prepared to see this through with me. It was comforting to know that she was there. It was also a relief that for right now, at this exact moment, I could believe that Sue cared about me and wouldn't abandon me no matter how terrible the memories were or how ashamed I felt. For right then, I could breathe more deeply, feel more relaxed and less alone.

Sue: Family reunion

I believe it's important to be available to clients in the middle of trauma work, so it's very hard when I have to say no. Elizabeth asked me today for a call on Saturday when I was to be away. That day, I was having 50 people for a family reunion in my vacation home. I knew that finding time to talk would be extremely difficult and that being emotionally available next to impossible. I told Elizabeth that I could talk with her on Friday, but Saturday was not possible. I briefly explained the situation, thinking that some explanation was required. I did not expect Elizabeth's reaction. In pre-trauma time, I would have received an "of course," and maybe a comment about finding another time. Today, she was furious at me. I know part of it was being reminded that I have family and that I was clearly putting them first. This was her nightmare: I would leave her behind and go off with my family. Although I knew this, I was shocked at the intensity of her anger and ultimately her hurt. As capable as she was of understanding the rational reasons behind my decision, her felt sense was one of abandonment and proof that her worst fears had been confirmed. It made me briefly question my decision, but ultimately, I held onto it and tried to stay with her despair. I wanted to defend my decision, but instead tried to hear her out on what my decision had felt like to her.

Finding ways of coping

As we became more familiar with Temporary Is Permanent, we found ways of countering its impact. We devised several unique ways of keeping a more "permanent" connection during our absences. For example, when Sue left she would give Elizabeth a piece of her piano music for Elizabeth to hold. Elizabeth could manage to trust that the music was important to Sue and would cause her to see Elizabeth again, at least to collect the music. The tragedy of this belief notwithstanding, the vignette illustrates the power of this gesture. Other techniques helped, as well. A colleague of Sue's, Ann, became a consistent back-up therapist and an extremely important way of managing Temporary is Permanent. It's important to note that the very nature of Temporary Is Permanent means it doesn't get better over time, since time and history have very little impact. We had to constantly battle it, talk about it and find ways of curbing its power.

The following vignettes show ways we battled Temporary Is Permanent.

Sue: Carrying her with me

I had been concerned about my upcoming vacation for some time. Because I was to be in Europe, I couldn't offer phone conversations with any confidence. I had to tell my clients that I would be unavailable for those two weeks. This morning I told Elizabeth, fearing the impact of that reality on her. For some time now, we had been aware of the need to counter Elizabeth's fears around my leaving in some way to help her keep our connection. In session, we talked about what would be possible in this new, more extreme situation. After some conversation,

Elizabeth decided that she wanted to bring two totems that had particular meaning to her and ask that I travel with one of them. She would keep the other one with her to remind her of my existence. She seemed relieved to have this option, and I was eager for anything that would help keep our connection real for her in my absence.

Elizabeth: Thank God for Ann!

I'd just seen Ann for the second time this week. Sue had been on vacation since last Friday. Even though I could talk to Sue while she was gone, I'd been trying to talk more with Ann instead. It was hard. I'd left Sue a number of messages since she'd been gone. We talked on the phone briefly three days after she left. It helped though to know that I had two appointments set up with Ann. She helped me to feel less ashamed about being in such a panic about Sue being gone. She also reassured me that Sue hadn't forgotten about me and would come back. Since I'd seen Ann every time Sue had gone away over the past few years, I knew Ann knew what was happening almost as much as Sue did. She didn't know everything, but she knew the very important pieces.

This week I came to new insights when I met with her. It was nice to get a different perspective. Of course, I would have traded a different perspective to have Sue around more. But it was comforting and very helpful to talk to Ann. Today I found myself struggling with admitting that I still panicked when Sue's on vacation. It took me awhile to be able to talk about it. One of the reasons I was so grateful for Ann was that I couldn't admit to anyone else the very deep and real panic I felt when Sue was gone. I was also very glad that since I could talk to Ann, I didn't have to ask Sue to do phone sessions with me when she was on vacation. I felt like such a loser when I had to ask Sue for extra time on her vacation. Now Sue got a bit of a break and I wasn't stranded emotionally. Ann seemed to understand how ashamed I felt about being so panicky when Sue was gone. It wasn't like the memories and flashbacks stopped once Sue was on vacation. These flashbacks and memories knocked me on my ass and sent me to suicidal feelings and drowned me in shame.

Elizabeth: Holding onto music book

Sue was back from vacation this morning. I was surprised at myself. I couldn't give her back the music book this time. I knew that the agreement was that she would give me a book of music to have while she was away, and when she returned, I would give it back to her. I couldn't today. Not yet. I wasn't totally sure why. It was very comforting for me to have the book. It had a lot of handwritten notes in the margins and within the music. The book was very old and I wondered if it was Sue's piano book when she was growing up or if it was from Sue's piano teaching days. Either way, it had her handwriting in it. I felt like I had a kind of journal of Sue's. I got to see the places that were hard either for her or a student or places in the music where special care must be taken.

Given that we had a deep connection through music, I guess it's not totally surprising that I felt very close to her through these music books. When Sue was gone – especially during her two-week vacations – I felt abandoned. I tried not to feel this way but usually I failed. I relied on the music books to read and to hold close to me to provide tangible evidence that Sue still existed and that I still existed for her. Even though she was back this morning, I wasn't ready to give that tangible evidence back to her. Sue seemed to understand. She wasn't disappointed or angry that I didn't return the music book. I explained that I wasn't ready to return it and she was fine with that. My connection to Sue always felt so tenuous. But I knew that her connection to music was very strong. She might refuse to see me again but she would contact me to get her music book returned. That ensured at least one more interaction. Maybe it meant that Sue wouldn't disappear from me until she recovered her music book.

Elizabeth: Playing for Sue

I did something today that took guts. But I did it. I was hoping that I could come up with a way that would help me to not freak out during the session before Sue's vacation. About a week ago, I decided that I wanted to sing John Denver's song "This Old Guitar" for her. I hauled my old guitar up to her office. When I walked into Sue's office and she saw my guitar, her eyes lit up and she smiled. I really wanted to sing for her, but most of the session went by before I could take my guitar out of the case. I'd been practicing all day – hoping my voice would hold and that my hands wouldn't miss the chords or strings as I played for her.

Well, things didn't go exactly as I had wished. My hands were steady enough. I played pretty well given that I haven't been playing my guitar with any regularity for 20 years. I was way too nervous for my voice to sound good, however. I sounded fair. A half hour before I sang for Sue, I was practicing and sounding really good – even for someone who hadn't been singing much for the past 20 years. But my nerves made my voice weak. Despite that, I was so glad I did it. I wanted to feel close to Sue, and sharing music – especially this song that speaks to how important this guitar has been for me – allowed me to feel that. She talked about what it meant to her for me to sing for her. She said it wasn't about performing, but about our connection.

Elizabeth: Holiday call from Sue

It was very difficult for me when I didn't get to see Sue because she was with her family on holidays. So many of our friends bitched about their families all year long but flock to be with family on holidays, leaving my wife and me to fend for ourselves. I think the same is true with therapists. We're supposed to lean on them and trust them and believe that we are important to them. But we're a small part of their world and not at all relevant. Maybe I shouldn't have been so bitter. I don't regularly see or talk to clients on holidays either. But I would agree to a short phone call with a client on a holiday if it would help the person.

However, I don't apply the same rule to myself. Being a psychologist didn't help me feel any better about how Sue abandoned me on holidays. It showed where I was in the hierarchy of her life – on the bottom. Sue told me this wasn't so. She explained that one kind of relationship doesn't cancel out other relationships. She cared about me just as much on holidays as she did on any other day.

"Sure, Sue," I thought. "Whatever you say. We don't get together on holidays or weekends. You have very definite times when you're available and when you're not."

I felt like a spoiled brat. I understood that Sue had a right to her own life and that it was ridiculous of me to feel jealous or abandoned. So today, I didn't know if I would be able to ask Sue to call me on Thanksgiving but somehow I managed. I waited until the end of a very long and agonizing session to ask. I couldn't find a way to ask her before then. I felt so unworthy of such requests. The internal cost of her refusing would have been very high. Before I asked I wondered if I would be able to continue to see Sue for therapy if she refused my request. This seemed like such a stupid thing, since my request seemed so out of line anyway. I asked her if we could talk for just five minutes on Thanksgiving. I explained that I knew that it was an unreasonable request. I was so afraid of what her response would be.

Thankfully, Sue agreed. She didn't seem put off by my request, either. She said she'd be happy to talk with me on Thanksgiving. I was shocked and relieved that Sue agreed to do this for me. We talked about how this wouldn't solve everything overnight but maybe it could help calm those parts of me that believed that I ceased to exist for Sue when I wasn't in her office or on the phone with her. I couldn't believe how much courage it took for me to ask her and how graciously and effortlessly she agreed. This was another example of taking huge amounts of time and energy to ask something of Sue that, for her, didn't seem to be a big deal. I'm not saying that she didn't know how huge this was for me. She knew — at least she expressed that. I meant that the differences in our realities could be very large. I was sweating and dreading her answer. I didn't think I had a right to even ask the question. Sue thought it was a reasonable request. It would have been nice if I'd come up with the courage to ask Sue to call me years sooner. It might have saved me a lot of anguish from the deep feelings of abandonment that choked me at each holiday.

On the way to healing

Like other dilemmas brought on by severe trauma memories, Temporary Is Permanent began to fade along with the memories. Elizabeth experienced a gradual lessening of the fear and confusion that accompanied Temporary Is Permanent, although this progress was not a linear progression. Also, much of Elizabeth's work in changing her responses to Sue's absence occurred when Sue was gone, resulting in a disconnect for Sue when Elizabeth "suddenly" was less in need of reassurance.

There were other factors for Elizabeth at this juncture as well: financial needs that pushed her to consider once-a-week therapy, less panic with Sue's absences and a general fatigue that left her feeling driven to get through the trauma material and on to a different relationship with Sue that would allow consideration of ending our therapy together.

Elizabeth: A slow change

Today was Friday. Sue had been gone for the past two weeks. I'd see her again on Tuesday. This was the first time since I started having new memories that I hadn't had a phone session with Sue or a face-to-face session with Ann in Sue's absence.

I wasn't totally sure why I had been able to wait. I'd tried very hard in the past to get through Sue's vacations without actual contact with her or Ann. This time it seemed the feeling of terror wasn't as strong. Overall, I wasn't living and breathing the kind of terror or agony that I'd been battling since the memories started. I also thought that I'd been able to use my brain more to keep myself calmer. When the fear grew, I was able to talk to myself and listen to Sue's messages to calm and comfort myself. I hoped this would continue. If the memories had really stopped, I might have been able to continue to find ways to tell myself that Sue still existed even when I didn't see her. I wasn't convinced of this. That's why the messages and totems helped. I still needed very concrete things to convince myself that Sue hadn't abandoned me. And that if she had, that I might be able to find a way to keep my sanity. I know that sounds dramatic. Unfortunately, that's exactly how it felt.

Everything was tentative. Nothing was certain. Things changed in a moment. For this vacation, however, I stood my own ground. I had been able to continue to function and stay calm without talking with Sue or Ann. I never thought I would see this day again!

Elizabeth: One session a week

Sue looked very surprised today when I told her I was cutting back to one session a week because I was taking a new half-time job that wouldn't allow me to have the time do our regular two sessions a week. A colleague I'd known for a few years approached me about joining a group of psychologists who practice out of a health clinic.

Cutting back to one session a week really scared me. I didn't feel ready for it. The problem is that I didn't think I'd ever feel "ready for it." I wasn't looking to change the amount of therapy I'd been doing. I wasn't even looking for more work. Over the many years since the memories started, I hadn't been able to even consider working in a setting that had no flexibility in scheduling. I couldn't reschedule a meeting or run out of one because I was having a flashback.

As I was considering this position, I realized that the flashbacks had actually slowed down. They didn't happen much anymore. When they did, they didn't tend to be as debilitating or last as long. I hadn't had new memories in a number of months, so I hadn't continued to be knocked off my feet every other day or week. My sleep had gotten a little bit better too. I wasn't plagued with constant nightmares. It didn't take me hours to get to sleep. Maybe things had started to get a little bit better without my noticing because I was still struggling with panic and so many unresolved feelings and beliefs.

I wanted this job but thought I might not be able to make it work. Perhaps I would have more flashbacks if I didn't see Sue twice a week. Perhaps I wouldn't be able to function without more constant support from her. I couldn't keep waiting to feel better or stronger or more confident. I had to do this despite feeling very afraid that the trauma would cripple me again without warning. I wasn't used to going into a new job with so many doubts about myself. No one knew how much I was struggling. But Sue knew. That helped me know I could go to her and not hide how terrified I was or how crazy I felt inside.

I was happy when Sue told me we could do more phone check-ins if I needed and that we could go back to two sessions a week if the job didn't work out. I felt ashamed that after all of this time I wasn't sure I'd be able to hang on to Sue's support if I didn't see her twice a week. I guessed I would find out.

Sue: Shock at decision to change schedule

Elizabeth came in today and dropped a bombshell. She let me know that her finances were in a tough space and she needed to find additional work to meet her needs. As a result, she wouldn't be able to see me twice a week as we had been doing for so long now. I'd been aware that the memories had finally stopped coming and as a result things have gotten better. We had stopped looking over our shoulder to see what might be lurking and had begun to settle in on working on some of the bigger issues about what she needed to feel healed enough from her trauma to move on. But I was shocked to hear her say so calmly that she was suddenly going to cut back half of our therapy time. Yet, I couldn't find any real reason to argue with her decision. She wasn't in any danger, her memories had stopped and she was functioning very well. I guess I just feel thrown by it. It wasn't a gradual process that we decided on together, and in fact, I hadn't even begun to think about ending our therapy. It also echoed what had happened so often: There was very little that was predictable about this process! I was glad that she felt ready to make this change and now I just had to find a way to adjust to the obvious shift in the level of intensity and connection we shared.

CHAPTER 5

SUICIDE IS ALWAYS AN OPTION

FEW EMOTIONS ARE more difficult to express or to hear about than suicidal thoughts and feelings. That level of despair is, thankfully, not part of most people's everyday experience, and often not the norm in the therapy office, either. In the context of a therapy relationship, discussions about suicidal thoughts and feelings evoke extreme discomfort for both the therapist and the client. As a therapist, there is never a more potent moment than when you realize that you literally are holding your client's survival within the context of a 50-minute conversation and on the foundation of whatever relationship you have built. That reality means that even if a client is "just" clinically depressed, most clinicians will periodically check for suicidal thoughts or impulses. When the answer to any of those exploratory questions is "yes," the therapist is likely to be on full alert. Most therapists believe an assessment needs to be made and potential action (hospitalization, contracts, medication, etc.) may need to be considered. The center of initiation often shifts to the therapist to direct the session and develop whatever plan may "need" to be made. For the client, having suicidal thoughts is even more terrifying: experiencing overwhelming feelings along with experiencing a helplessness to change them. It can be shocking at another level to find oneself suddenly at odds with such a basic belief as the will to live, and it is almost always a shameful admission. The despair is completely overwhelming.

Although it is possible for a trauma survivor never to experience suicidal thoughts, it's not unusual for someone with a history of trauma to struggle with suicidal thoughts in a variety of ways and levels of intensity. During "pre-trauma time," although she might have still considered herself a "trauma survivor," Elizabeth never experienced suicidal thoughts or feelings. She was very much connected to the losses in her life and tuned into the difficulties ahead as she worked on several life dilemmas. She experienced great sadness and had moments of despair that her family was unable to affirm her experience, punished her for telling the truth and made it impossible to maintain a connection with them. However, none of these powerful feelings led her to suicidal thoughts.

Elizabeth's first suicidal thoughts seemed to come literally out of nowhere and shocked both of us. In retrospect, it is obvious that she was anticipating a flood of new memories that had just begun to surface. Once the memories became clear, we both had something to point to as a means to put these new thoughts into context. That helped, but it still felt like a crisis, and we both assumed it would pass, or at least ebb and flow. That belief helped us initially deal with the crisis through negotiation, check-in calls and extra sessions. We were, perhaps, blissfully ignorant of the process we had started, but in the moment, the extra reassurance that those gestures provided was enough to reassure both of us.

Within a relatively short time, however, we began to struggle with the reality that this was not a short-term crisis and we would have to find ways of "being" with these thoughts on an ongoing basis. We both had to acknowledge, over and over again, that struggling with suicidal thoughts was not a crisis that would fade away and that suicidal thoughts and urges would be with us, as a constant companion, throughout our time together. How we managed these thoughts changed over time as Sue struggled with how to address Elizabeth's strong need to die that was engaged in a battle with her stubbornness to live.

While Elizabeth coped with her internal battle, Sue struggled with her own dilemma. Sue strongly believes that the therapist needs to find ways of connecting to the client's experience by following her lead and trying to find a place of empathic connection. Although there are always hits and misses in that process of tuning in with a client, the goal is to stay with the client, without leading, until some real understanding is achieved. It was also important to Sue to approach Elizabeth without judging her symptoms or using them to put her in a diagnostic box. She tried to stay open and respectful, and harbor no preconceived ideas about what needed to happen at any given time. She tried to be flexible and willing to shift gears in the moment, following Elizabeth's lead and trusting that Elizabeth knew best what would be helpful.

These beliefs, which we ultimately understood as shared, sometimes came into sharp conflict with "proper clinical protocol" in the face of powerful suicidal thoughts and feelings, which required a shift from that stance. Because of the extreme intensity and very real danger of this particular "symptom," following a frame that prohibits any leading of the client is challenging. It would be far easier, at least in the moment, to shift to a preprogrammed stance that would ensure as much safety at a concrete level as possible, leaving the "relationship" to later. Thus, there were times Sue gave in to these well-established protocols and explored the option of hospitalization, causing Elizabeth to feel unheard while handling extremely powerful feelings – certainly not a helpful process. At the same time, those thoughts and feelings had to be taken seriously and other plans had to be made to help Elizabeth keep herself safe.

Our ability to navigate this dilemma relied almost completely on our shared belief in our relationship as the most reliable resource. Ultimately, concern for immediate safety had to be balanced with the need to be with Elizabeth, to understand the despair that speaks of suicide, and our belief that the power of our relationship to tune in with those feelings was far more helpful than safety protocols. There certainly were moments as the intensity of suicidal thoughts increased when the hospitalization option reappeared, but for the majority of our time together, it was our relationship and how we trusted each other that allowed us both to survive the Suicide Is Always an Option nightmare.

In these vignettes, we hope to give a glimpse into our evolution of dealing with suicidal thoughts, feelings and plans. We have both wondered if it is really possible to portray the enormous draining power of persistent suicidal thoughts on a relationship, and have concluded that it probably is not. However, it is worth looking at these vignettes to glean some idea of what our process was over our eight years discovering and working with Suicide is Always an Option. The vignettes provide one of the strongest testimonies to our core set of shared beliefs that being authentically with the client's place in the moment and in the therapeutic relationship, trying to find a way of resonating with the client's felt experience, following her lead and being with her experience as much as possible, is the best, and ultimately only, path to healing. We have tried to provide an honest picture of the ups and downs of our experience feeling like a client who was always on the "brink" and as a therapist who walked with a client who was always considering suicide.

It is important not to give the impression that these powerful suicidal thoughts and feelings were not directly addressed. Sue was focused on not shaming Elizabeth's feelings and thoughts, and was committed to understanding her experience as much as possible. While Elizabeth fought with the hospitalization issue throughout our time together, that was never the focus. However, not hospitalizing, not judging or interpreting and not imposing an agenda did not mean we did not attend these powerful feelings. We developed a wide variety of ways of being with Elizabeth's suicidal thoughts and feelings. When Elizabeth let Sue know that she was suicidal, Sue would often ask her about ways Elizabeth knew that would help keep her safe. Sometimes, it looked like a conversation that tried to clarify Elizabeth's experience, or it looked like play time or shared silence. It sometimes led to our "playing" with GI Joes or Legos, drawing or simply being together in sadness, anger, terror or any other feeling that she was immersed in.

Out of these conversations developed several ways that we used throughout the years to battle the despair of suicide. We would often schedule extra sessions, check-in calls that sometimes were messages left back and forth and sometimes brief conversations or messages that Sue would leave on Elizabeth's voice mail that she could listen to as she needed. Sometimes we would plan together ways for Elizabeth to stay connected with her life and "prescribe" time with her friends, either in person or on the phone. For us, our shared love of music provided a rich source of comfort in suicidal times and we used this in a variety of ways. At times, Elizabeth brought in music to share in a session as a way of letting Sue know how she was feeling. At other times, Elizabeth would ask Sue to play the piano at home for her and just let her know that she did so and thought of her as she played. Sometimes Sue would share pieces of music whose lyrics seemed especial relevant to what we were talking about. Following Elizabeth's lead in the session led to some nonverbal ways of confirming our connection that helped battled the suicidal feelings. Sue would often move her chair closer to Elizabeth, and hold her hand. When images surfaced or toys appeared, it meant using those images or toys as the language of suicidal thoughts, without interpretation or comment.

Writing these vignettes was difficult for both of us. Elizabeth found herself full of regret and sorrow for making the people closest to her fear for her life for so long. Sue found herself revisiting her struggle to forgo the "safest" clinical response of pushing for hospitalization to be with Elizabeth in her despair. She felt some regret for the times she left that stance with Elizabeth and reverted to discussing hospitalization or medication options, as her own anxiety and deep concern sometimes pushed her to do.

The first incident

As we previously mentioned, Elizabeth did not have any suicidal thoughts or feelings in pre-trauma time. Our first experience with suicidal ideation seemed to come from nowhere and ushered in trauma time before we really understood we were there. Elizabeth's new memories had not yet surfaced when the suicidal thoughts began.

Elizabeth: Out of the blue

Yesterday, I found myself calling Sue while sitting in my car at a local park. I wasn't sure what else I should do. These feelings came out of the blue. How could I have become suicidal overnight? What prompted this? Why was this urge so strong? My life had been stressful lately, but nothing that should turn my thoughts so strongly to those guns that Ellen keeps in the attic. Nothing had happened that warranted this kind of obsession. I sat in the car too terrified to go home. I left a message for Sue describing what was happening and where I was. I wasn't sure what I was going to do if Sue didn't call back before I had to leave the park.

The cell phone rang and I was relieved to hear Sue on the other end. We talked about how I could stay safe. She asked me to tell Ellen what was going on and to ask her to get rid of the guns and ammunition. I didn't want to tell Ellen, but I was scared that I wouldn't be able to stop myself from shooting myself in the head if I find the guns. I'd gone from no suicidal thoughts to a plan and a strong need to do something lethal. It didn't feel like a cry for help. There was a part of me that really wanted to be dead. But there was another part of me that didn't. I told Sue my plan to tell Ellen despite the ramifications. Sue asked me to call her later to let her know how I was. We scheduled an extra session for the next day and stayed in phone contact throughout today. I was relieved that Sue believed that this is as serious as it feels.

Sue: Our first negotiation

Last session was the first hint I had that Elizabeth had any suicidal thoughts. She briefly mentioned them, but easily came to the conclusion that she was not in any danger of hurting herself. She was pretty embarrassed even to talk about it and seemed eager to deal with them quickly. I was surprised: There didn't seem to be any sudden crisis that precipitated these feelings, and although we had been discussing some difficult issues, none was dramatically new or traumatic. So I was really thrown off guard when Elizabeth called today and let me know she was feeling suicidal. She reported it to me as if a completely disenfranchised voice inside her needed to speak, despite her extreme distaste for its message. It took a while for her to tell me because she was so embarrassed; she apologized to me for being "so messed up." She was angry but she said she also was scared. So was I. It looked like our last session was just the "warm-up," and now we were really in it.

I got a little more detailed with her by asking the questions I had been taught to do to make a "suicide assessment," such as asking if she had a plan, what it was, were there any beliefs that she saw suicide as an untenable act, were there other symptoms, and what was the depth of her suicidal thinking, while trying also to absorb and reflect this rather sudden expression of such deep despair. I wasn't prepared for her plan. Apparently, her partner is in the Reserves, and there is both a gun and ammunition in the house. Phew! This was not a commonplace situation for me. There are lots of potential suicide plans, but any plan that involves a gun has the most chance of being fatal – a real red flag.

We talked for a long time, and Elizabeth agreed to ask her partner to remove the gun and hide both the gun and the ammunition separately. Normally, at this point, I would consider hospitalization, and we talked about it. However, Elizabeth seemed to have calmed down fairly quickly and she convincingly assured me that she could keep herself safe with our plan in place. She was so horrified that the suicidal thoughts had even entered her head, and so relieved to have my help to manage them that I was pretty confident we didn't need to go any further. I knew that we would meet the next day and talk further about this. We set up phone check-ins every couple of hours until then, to give her a continued connection to me, as well as to reassure me that she could keep to her promise and maintain her safety.

After she hung up, my body reverberated for a few minutes from the intensity of our conversation. We were in new territory – a place that I would prefer not to be. I hated feeling that I so literally had someone's life in my hands, even though I was painfully aware that I really couldn't keep Elizabeth or anyone else from hurting themselves. The decision I made today gave me a lot more power than I would have wanted, and I was already a little nervous that I didn't take it all the way to hospitalization. I hoped strongly that her own distaste for these new thoughts would keep her safe until we saw each other the next day.

Early stages

Sessions when we discussed suicide were never easy. These vignettes highlight the difficulty for both of us when Elizabeth was suicidal and had to discuss very specific suicidal plans with Sue. When the plan was very specific, it was difficult for Sue to stay with Elizabeth's experience without feeling the need to take steps to ensure Elizabeth's safety. When Elizabeth's plans were less specific, and with the help of time together that provided us an increased sense of mutual trust, Sue could spend much more time trying to resonate with Elizabeth's experience of suicidal despair without feeling the same urgency around safety plans as she felt at the emergence of the suicidal thoughts and feelings. These vignettes illustrate the beginning of the suicidal ideation when the dilemma of hospitalization vs. "being with the client" was at its sharpest.

Sue: Hospitalization dilemma

Near the beginning of the session today, Elizabeth told me just how suicidal she was feeling. I asked all the usual questions to assess the level of danger she was in and was shocked to hear her go into some detail about her plan to kill herself. She had already purchased a hose for the exhaust pipe of her car, duct tape and a clamp. She knew of a time that she could get to her garage and be alone. She truly believed she had no other way out and was desperate to do this. We spent a lot of time talking, and I went back and forth between assessing just how dangerous the situation was and trying to let her talk about how she was feeling without "fixing" it. The fact that this was not only a plan, but also a plan with all the ingredients made it especially urgent. Eventually, she agreed to take the items back to the store, and I believed her. However, the level of her despair was so deep that I was frightened that she would find another way to harm herself. I couldn't get out of my head what my training required me to do at this point: If there's a clear plan, hospitalize. So, I reluctantly brought up hospitalization.

We talked about it at some length. Elizabeth was distraught that I would even consider hospitalization, and had some really viable reasons why it was so abhorrent to her. As an experienced therapist, she knew exactly what hospitalization meant and was adamant that she wouldn't ever consider it. It was clear that involuntary hospitalization was my only option. However, complicating that distasteful option was the reality that Elizabeth knew exactly what to say to hospital personnel to either avoid hospitalization against her will or at least to get out of an involuntary hospitalization at the first opportunity. Realistically, any hospitalization would be no more than 72 hours – a temporary fix that in no way measured up to the enormity of her suicidal leanings. Elizabeth also had well-founded concerns that a hospitalization in the community where she practiced could do serious damage to her professional self, making the thought of hospitalization even more abhorrent and risky. The shame of even considering that was overwhelming to her. All in all, it just wasn't a useful option.

There were other reasons against hospitalization that were especially compelling to me. "Dumping" Elizabeth on the hospital risked proving her worse fears: that telling me about her trauma would mean that I could no longer be in relationship with her. It would confirm her belief that I couldn't handle hearing about her despair. It would mean that her fears were true: once she was "known to me," the reality of her experience as a "throw-away person" (her repeated self-assessment) would manifest. I also had serious doubts that hospitalization would solve anything. Certainly, she would be "safe" for a very brief period, but then we would be back in my office (if she hadn't fired me by then) dealing with the same overwhelming emotions with the addition of a shameful experience that I had imposed on her.

So, she convinced me that hospitalization was not a viable choice, and I retreated to a stance that she asked for: listening to her and trying to understand what it was like to be feeling that level of pain. I was exhausted by the end of this session and not a little scared that I had once again taken too many risks, essentially with her life. I had a gut sense that she could hold to her promises to me, and that our regular check-ins between today and our next session would be a powerful tool to remind her of our relationship. The clinician in her knew the risk I was taking, and let me know that she was grateful to me for not rigidly following protocol. Both of us knew I was putting my head on the block by not insisting on hospitalization, and that helped reassure me that Elizabeth would honor her promise to me. Unfortunately, I couldn't reassure myself completely, and was tremendously relieved later when Elizabeth kept her promise of regular check-ins and reported feeling better as she did so.

Elizabeth: It happened again

As I walked into Sue's office, I felt heavy and afraid of the topic I had to talk about – again. Sometimes I felt Sue's understanding and love when I brought up suicidal thoughts. Other times she jumped to suicide contracts and asked about hospitalization. I wished she would listen to my experience and be with me in the pain and uncertainly. Sometimes I could voice the pain. Sometimes I was honest with her about how close I came, again, to hurting myself. Other times I was too ashamed to let on how much I had been struggling with wanting to kill myself. It took me the whole session to tell Sue the story of this particular incident.

I explained to Sue that last night I stood in the kitchen with a knife to my throat. The dialogue that played in my head was between life and death. Back and forth I went:

Do it. Just get it over with. Ellen won't be home for hours. Plenty of time to die from bleeding to death.

I don't want to.

Do it.

No, I'm afraid. I don't want to hurt Ellen like that.

Ellen hates you. Everyone hates you.

No, Ellen and Sue would be devastated.

No, Sue would be relieved. She wouldn't care at all.

No, I don't think that's right. But this agony will never go away. It will never get any better. This is what I am doomed to live out.

End it here and you will find peace.

No, I know the devastation of the aftermath of suicide. Ellen doesn't deserve this. She'll find me. She'll never be the same.

Maybe she won't even care.

No, that's not true. She will care. She will be devastated. I can't do this to her.

I put the knife back into the drawer. Tears were streaming down my cheeks. I was overcome by pain and remorse for having had a knife to my throat, for having come so close again.

"What stopped you from using the knife?" Sue asked. I told her the truth. "I really don't know." Not a satisfying or comforting answer for either of us. I told her that I often thought: "I don't do this to the people I love." I was humiliated and ashamed of myself. If I wasn't so afraid of not being able to withstand the suicidal impulse the next time this happened (and I knew it will happen again), I wouldn't talk to Sue about it. If I wasn't afraid that I could stop myself from acting on my suicidal urges next time I wouldn't talk to Sue about it at all. Sue asked, "Why didn't you call me? We could have done check-in calls." Again I answered, "I don't know." But then I admitted, "I'm frustrated. I didn't want to call. I wanted to kill myself."

"You're still here. Some part of you wanted to live," Sue responded.

Sometimes I was so angry with Sue's line of thinking on this. I didn't think there was a part of me that wanted to live. I thought I was a coward. If I had had the guts, I would have been dead years ago. "Don't talk to me about a part of me that wants to live. Talk to me about a part of me that is too afraid to end my own suffering," I thought. In that moment I felt more alone and desperate.

After I explained this to Sue, she gently commented that it must be awful to feel so much agony that dying is the only way out. I relaxed little bit. I didn't have to defend or explain myself. I didn't feel so alone and I was able to breathe a little deeper. I had just a tiny bit of hope that my connection with Sue in my despair might help me to withstand the next onslaught of suicidal thoughts. With each new incident I felt more at risk of actually completing the latest version of "suicide du jour." But, like today, when Sue could let me know that she was trying to understand my experience, at least I was not alone in my questioning.

Relying on our connection

After the early response to Elizabeth's suicidal thoughts and feelings, we began to rely most heavily on a core set of beliefs that informed Sue's way of doing therapy, which we ultimately discovered were very much in line with Elizabeth's clinical views. We both believe that these shared beliefs made it possible for Elizabeth to stay in therapy with Sue, and ultimately to heal.

The following vignettes illustrate both the difficulties in following these beliefs, and the relief for each of us when we were able to achieve that connection.

Sue: Letting go to be with Elizabeth

Near the end of today's session, after long periods of painful silences, Elizabeth again admitted just how suicidal she was feeling. I felt my stomach drop and my anxiety rise. It is such a familiar place, and one that I have agonized over since Elizabeth's suicidal ideation surfaced.

Having long since given up hospitalization as the ultimate fall back, I had begun to rely increasingly on Elizabeth's strong conviction that she didn't want to hurt the people around her, primarily her partner and me, by that act. So, here I was, anxiously leaving old dictates that implore me to follow all the clinical protocols, to sit with the reality of a suicidal person who is in a unique relationship with me. Today, I was very clear and decided to just be with her again and completely avoid the "easier" route of suicide contract or hospitalization. It was still so hard for me. I've sat with suicidal clients before and even had to hospitalize a few whose depression was so overwhelming that they had no capacity to assure me or themselves that they could stay safe.

At other times, as with Elizabeth, I had worked to maintain a hold on her will to live through the power of the therapeutic relationship. But Elizabeth's had gone on for so long that I found myself unwillingly sharing some of her terror that these feelings would never change. I cared deeply for this person, and felt such connection to her in so many ways, but we had completely opposite realities at this time when it came to the sanctity of life.

Underneath all this despair, I knew that Elizabeth shared many of my beliefs; but in the moment she couldn't access that but stood firmly in her belief that she had no reason to live. Normally, when I sit with a client, I always look for some place in myself or in my own life experience that can resonate with the client's story so I can better empathize and be with her in her experience. The suicidal thoughts were tough for me. I have never been suicidal, and can scarcely imagine getting to the point of even considering it. However, I have a strong belief in the right to die, and have had a Living Will for a long time. I found that a place of connection, and tried to imagine myself in such physical pain that death seemed like a relief. Once there, I had a slightly better understanding of Elizabeth's story and could tolerate hearing it more easily. The trick here, of course, was that I could never sanction suicide as a choice for Elizabeth. I truly believed that her trauma "illness" was not life-threatening and that she would have a full recovery, much different than a terminally ill patient.

Elizabeth talked for the entire session about how impossible it was for her to see herself as worthy of life, and I tried to stay with her, silencing the programmed part of my brain that insisted I consider hospitalization as the ultimate path to safety. It was hard, but once I had made up my mind to stay with her, I at least had a clear path. She cried, I felt like crying and the session ended. We agreed to talk several times tomorrow, and Elizabeth seemed relieved to having been heard. However, I couldn't say that I felt relief. It was an exhausting place to be. I always had at least a 15-minute break between the end of Elizabeth's session and my next client. I was especially grateful for the break today, and found myself sitting in silence for most of that time, letting myself be with the enormity of the experience I had just shared with Elizabeth.

I also felt nervous, and hoped that I had not been foolish in not getting at least a verbal contract from her today. Every bone in my body wanted to believe in the strength of our connection, but I never felt it was so absolute that it could not be broken in a moment of overwhelming despair. I fervently hoped that this was not such a moment. I talked with myself, arguing what I knew: if I hospitalized Elizabeth every time suicide was in the air, we would rarely be in the office. This was not a "suicidal crisis" as it is had often been termed in my training. This was an ongoing crisis that was always with us. We could no more stop the trauma work than stop a speeding train with wishes. Suicidal thoughts were an integral part of that trauma work and they were going to be with us. We would have to find a way to work with these thoughts, continuing to pay serious attention to them, but not allow them to short circuit what was most critical: our relationship, with the suicidal feelings as an integral part. I was going to have to continue to let go of the "protocols" and be with Elizabeth in what we had come to call "the pits."

Elizabeth: Sue not judging me

Today I had a very hard time describing to Sue how suicidal I'd been feeling. It took most of the session to get the words out. But when I did I was so relieved when Sue didn't judge me for having these ongoing struggles. I was afraid she would tell me that I could change if I just tried harder. Often when she pushed – or even mentioned – hospitalization or safety plans I thought she was judging me and pushing me aside. In those moments I didn't think she wanted to hear my pain and struggle. Today she didn't mention contracts or hospitalization. I was able to delve deeper into the despair I felt that fueled suicidal thoughts, the shame I felt for having suicidal thoughts and urges and the frustration and anger I felt about having this battle at all.

When Sue listened to my pain like this and didn't interject her own agenda, I felt very close to her. I judged myself so harshly, and rightly so: I'd screwed up so many things and I was hurting the people I love with my depression and despair. But today I could give myself a break because Sue gave me a break. Maybe she generally doesn't judge me as harshly as I feared she did. But today I experienced her compassion and love for me as she sat with me and listened to my struggle. It was still hard to communicate. I hated myself for being so weak. I wanted to kill myself so I could end this misery. I didn't see another way out.

Today I spoke about how much I wanted to kill myself and how much I hated myself because I couldn't go through with it. Sue accepted me and didn't judge me for this battle or self-hatred or wanting to commit suicide. She listened and seemed to deeply feel the pain I expressed. Her acceptance and nonjudgmental attitude today lessened the pain. I wasn't so alone. Previously she tried to make me feel better or change my thinking, I often ended up feeling more alone and desperate. Not today, though. Today I was able to describe the struggle in great detail. Today I could believe that Sue was on my side and that really helped to lessen the struggle. I hoped this reprieve could last a while. I was so weary. I needed Sue's acceptance, and it was very healing when I felt it so strongly.

A different language helps

In the following vignettes, we describe two examples of using images, one concrete and one imaginary, that allowed us to be with each other without directly speaking of suicide. In the third example, we illustrate that an authentic gesture from Sue at Elizabeth's request contributed to our connection at a critical time. All three examples clearly were focused on the despair that was the source of Elizabeth's suicidal ideation, and came at Elizabeth's suggestion, but in none of these examples were suicidal thoughts discussed or the actions interpreted.

Sue: The despairing soldier speaks

For several months now, Elizabeth occasionally brought GI Joe toys to our session. She found that using the dolls and the obvious war theme had been helpful to her. Often, one of the soldiers was wounded and in desperate need of rescue and care. At different stages, there had been a doctor who provided care and other soldiers who came and went in the story. The story had yet to have a happy ending.

Today she brought them in with one of the soldiers covered in "bloody" bandages with "broken bones," who was "fighting for his life." She saw the soldier as all alone, critically wounded and in need of rescue. She despaired that one of the other soldiers was "lost in the woods" and not able to help. There was another doll who had taken the role of doctor in previous sessions, so I asked if the doctor could at least tend to the wounds while he waited for rescue. She said the doctor cared, but didn't know if he could save the soldier. But then, with my help, she spent some time unwinding the bandages and the splints and tending to this injured soldier. The "lost" soldier then appeared and told the first soldier that there was very little hope of being rescued. After some talking, that soldier offered to sing to the injured soldier, and that seemed to help. Although it was clear to both of us that this was a thinly disguised metaphor for the despair that often leads to suicidal ideation, we never spoke of that, and continued to discuss the rescue possibilities for this soldier. At the end of the session, she asked that I keep the GI Joes at the office "for safekeeping," and I agreed. She had prepared a "bed" for the injured soldier and we made room on my closet shelf for the dolls.

As sessions in which suicidal ideation was front-and-center, this was a relatively "easy" one for me. Somehow, in the midst of our struggle to be able to talk about the constant suicidal despair, and talking about whether Elizabeth could find a way to trust me enough to be with her in that despair, having an entire session devoted to these "dolls" avoided speaking to that issue directly and gave us the freedom to talk about her fears without complication. Working with the dolls today let me know how hard it was for Elizabeth to hold any hope of "rescue" from the enormous pain that she was in, as well as how insufficient the rescue operation appears. I suppose I could have interpreted that to mean me, and that was a reasonable interpretation, but it also underlined her global fears in a clearly understandable way, allowing me to be empathic with the despairing "soldier" rather than hearing her despair in the form of anger or hopelessness directly at me.

Sue: Music to soothe the despair when words don't work

I had just hung up the phone with Elizabeth, who was feeling an enormous amount of grief. When she was not in the midst of new memories and sorting out just what actually happened, she sometimes could stand back and take in the enormity of what her traumatic history meant to the story of her life. Today was one of those days. She had not had any contact with her family, except her sister, in five years, and though she had worked hard to create a new family with her partner and a community with her friends, it wasn't the same. Christmas was only a couple of weeks away, and she was faced again with the fragility of a community of friends competing with the pull of families when holidays are involved. She just found out that some friends with whom she had hoped to spend some of the Christmas holiday were leaving to be with their families. That news hit her hard and led her to talk about what she missed. All her values told her that family is most important. Everything she believed would have her be committed to spending time with her family of origin. But she just couldn't. Instead, she reminisced today about Ping Pong games between the cousins in her family, and large gatherings at Thanksgiving and Christmas. She laughed at pet nicknames and favorite jokes shared between branches of her family.

As she recalled more memories, she was also more and more aware of the meaning of some of the decisions and choices in her life. She knew now that her frequent moves early in her adult life, which made no sense at the time and cost her dearly, kept her from getting too close to people or becoming too successful. The motivations were unconscious at the time, but they were there, doing the dirty work for her abusers and short-changing her life experiences over and over again. The grief was boundless. At the end of our phone conversation, she asked me to play something for her on the piano and to think of her as I played. She didn't need to hear it; she just wanted to know that I would do that for her. I felt a little like being asked to pray for someone, though she never said that. I knew almost immediately when she asked me that I would play the opening of a Beethoven Sonata, called "les Adieux." It has always been a favorite of mine, and evokes for me a beautiful statement of grief. I hung up the phone and went right to the piano, played for her and wept.

The despair that comes with losing yourself

The next vignettes highlight the client's confusion arising from losing one's identity in the midst of trauma memories, while the therapist holds both realities. In that realm, there is no "shared reality" that seems like such a valuable part of any relationship. For us, we labeled this disparity as the "old Elizabeth" and the "new Elizabeth" to delineate the complete divide between who Elizabeth knew herself to be before the trauma was remembered, and the "other person" she knew herself to be after her trauma took her by full force. There were times when our discussions of the "old Elizabeth" and the "new Elizabeth" seemed to resonate for both of us, and Elizabeth would ask to be reminded of who she was underneath all the trauma, finding that reminder helpful. The first vignette describes how Sue's knowledge of that disparity and her willingness to reconnect Elizabeth to the "old Elizabeth" were sometimes useful.

On a deeper level, there also were times when referencing the "old Elizabeth" caused a sense of disconnection and even shame for Elizabeth, coupled with her deep belief and regret that she could never reclaim that person. These vignettes give an example of both experiences.

Sue: Remembering the "old Elizabeth"

Elizabeth talked today again about just how suicidal she was feeling. In tears, she despaired at having nothing to live for, no hope that she would ever escape from these feelings and no belief that there was anything to her beyond these terrifying trauma memories. She saw herself as "a throw-away person," "disgusting," "worthless" and "pathetic." She went on and on, describing herself in subhuman terms. In the past, we talked about the "old Elizabeth" and the "new Elizabeth." She could sometimes remember her "old" self, but it was both hard and painful, and it was as if it was a story about someone else. She despaired that she could ever be that person again. The experience of reliving her trauma made it feel like those qualities of self could never be re-captured.

I'm not sure what triggered this in me, but I really wanted to remind her of who she "was" and who I still know her to be. I told her how sad I was that she couldn't believe any part of her that existed before this trauma and began to remind her of who I still believed her to be. I talked for a few minutes about the "old Elizabeth," the funny, charming, intelligent person I knew. I reminded her of her skills as a writer, a therapist, a musician and a friend. I talked about her social justice values and her spirituality. Although Elizabeth had let me know that what she most needed when she was suicidal was for me to listen and try to understand her experience as much as I could, the switch from that stance was helpful to her today. She became tearful and said how much she missed being that person. She could hardly remember her, but knew I was telling her the truth. She was reassured by my belief that the "old Elizabeth" was still there and that I believed we would find her again. She said she was relieved and left the session with just a little lighter step. I was relieved, too.

I knew it was risky to leave my stance and assert my own agenda, and it probably came more from my own fatigue and feelings of helplessness than from a sound clinical understanding of what was most needed. But sometimes, the impulses between people in relationship aren't easily categorized and this time, intuition worked. I felt a little like I was pleading with her to remember, but perhaps I was also busy reminding myself. It was a little crazy-making for me to sit with her in these moments and keep in my mind the very solid picture of her that I carried that was so radically different from the one she presented to herself. It sustained me most of the time, but it could also lead me to some of the same places where Elizabeth found herself: those terrified moments when it was hard to have any hope that anything would ever get better. I was very glad that Elizabeth and I could essentially reassure each other of the person we were fighting to reclaim.

Elizabeth: I'll never be me again

Sometimes Sue told me that she knew the "old Elizabeth" was still inside of me. I told Sue today that the "old Elizabeth" was dead. The person who had a strong faith in the goodness of the universe had ceased to exist. The person who could easily and joyfully pursue music lessons and performances is gone. The optimist, the person who believed in the goodness of this world and that, somehow, good would eventually prevail over evil, was dust. I missed that person. I missed having a solid foundation on which to stand, one that helped me weather the storms, trials, uncertainties and unfairness of life. I wanted to feel courageous again. I wanted to know in the depths of my being that my suffering was not in vain. I missed being happy and outgoing. Maybe one day I wouldn't be depressed but I doubted that I would ever again be joyful. I had lost too much in this retelling and discovery of truth. The Truth didn't "set me free." It crippled me.

I shouted at Sue, "I am broken!" After calming down, I explained that I might not be broken in physical terms but my spirit is crushed. Once my spirit was crushed, any sense of myself vanished also. I explained that I now determined what my beliefs were by observing myself. For example, if I listened carefully to a client or friend that meant that I valued connection. If I gave some change to the homeless man on the corner, then I had some generosity of spirit. If I liked to go someplace I'd never been on vacation, then that I was adventurous.

Now, this shitty "healing" process, which had revealed the level of my abuse, crushed who I was and replaced it with someone who knew little of herself. Today Sue didn't argue with me about this. She reminded me of things I could still do – the roles I still performed successfully. This helped a bit. Still, she thought that we were "reclaiming" who I was. I knew that wasn't true. My old self was dead. I was working hard to find a new self. I didn't know who I would be. I wasn't even sure I'd ever find a solid foundation again on which to build. The universe was now unpredictable and so was I. No matter who I was now, I grieved for the person I had been and the beliefs I lost in this process. Sometimes – often, really – this loss robbed me of any desire to live. I believed that my death was the only thing that would bring me relief from this agony of spirit and the loss of myself and any trust I had in the universe.

Authentic relationship

By now, we had spent years reliving the horrors of Elizabeth's traumatic history, and like most people in relationships born in trauma, we had both a deep affection for each other as well as a wariness born from sporadic periods of frustration and disappointment. It was anxiety provoking for both of us when we got caught in places of misunderstanding, but by now, we also felt some sense of trust in each other to be as honest and genuine as we could be in order to sort through what had surfaced. Sometimes it would take weeks or months to fully understand what was going on, or sometimes just a session, but we knew we would get there eventually. That said, the process still was exhausting for both of us and called for unending patience and trust in both each other and the process of therapy itself. In that process, the "normal therapeutic roles" faded, and along with our belief in the need to be authentic came some moments of authenticity that surprised, embarrassed and ultimately had more power than all the other experiences had put together.

The following vignettes are examples of the "real" part of our relationship having far more power than any more expected part of a therapeutic relationship and how an unplanned disclosure from Sue provided the authentic proof of her concern that Elizabeth needed to begin to shake loose from the thoughts of suicide.

Sue: In it together

We talked so much about the despair that speaks of suicide that I felt sometimes that there was nothing I could say or do that would have any impact on Elizabeth, or would be of any help at all. Today's session started out that way. Elizabeth came in feeling intense and relentless despair and began speaking of it to me. She really wasn't sure she could manage the overwhelming emotions in a way that would keep her safe. I did my usual juggling act between trying to tune into her despair while also working with her to see what we could do to help keep her safe. This was familiar to both of us and we went along in this way for some time. However, at one point, we shifted to talking about our process itself. It was excruciating for both of us and, even though I think we were both aware of the toll it takes on the other, it was tremendously relieving to talk about it with Elizabeth.

Elizabeth let me know how she agonized each time she felt she had to bring up suicidal ideation, weighing the need to talk about it against the cost. Part of it was that it gave her enormous internal pain to have to speak of something that felt like a personal indictment of her character. She deplored that she was in that place, she hated that she had to speak of it to me and she was appalled that she was putting her partner, me and others who love her, in this terrifying place. The shame of speaking of suicidal thoughts and feelings, much less actual plans, was overwhelming: she "should" be able to deal with this herself, She "should" be able to resource her history of valuing life and stop herself from these thoughts. The other part of her dilemma was that she knew by bringing up suicidal despair we would focus on that in the session, often to the detriment of other issues that felt at least as urgent. Once that topic was broached, we gave it our full attention.

I also let Elizabeth know some of my dilemmas when we were in the suicidal place. I told her how I really understood that she needed me to just listen to her and to try to understand what her experience was like. I let her know that I, too, realized that there was no guaranteed "fix" for the place that we were in, even though I desperately wished for one. I told her how hard it was to hear the depth of her pain and feel so helpless in the face of it. I told her I trusted our relationship and that I trusted her to call me, but I was sometimes scared that she just wouldn't be able to do it – and that was a terrifying thought that haunted me.

It felt like we were both stepping back from our normal roles in this conversation to define our individual experience of shame as we navigated Suicide Is Always an Option. Suicide became a third member of the party and we could share our mutual shame around trying to be with it, understand it and deal with it. It felt a little like we were reaffirming that we were on the same side, struggling with our own demons around this issue, with the powerful resource of our connection in mind. Our relationship was front and center today, and it was very reassuring to me, and, I think, to Elizabeth. I felt like an important door had been opened, and I was sure we would talk about this again.

Elizabeth: Losing sleep

We did a phone session today because Sue was on vacation. I felt raw during the call. I could hardly talk to her. I just had another bad day and night of suicidal thoughts. Sue had asked me the day before to call her to let her know how I was doing. I couldn't do it. The last time she saw me and we talked before she left for vacation, I was very caught in the pain of memories and I wanted to die. She asked me to call her so that she knew I was still able to keep myself safe. I couldn't call her.

From the way this session went, I would say that Sue and I were both very frustrated with each other. At one point Sue said in exasperation, "I can't keep this up. I couldn't sleep at all last night because I was so worried about you." She was quick to add that there were other things on her mind as well. However, she reiterated that the main reason for her sleepless night was that she did not know if I would kill myself that evening. I was shocked to hear her say this. For some reason, knowing this immediately pierced through any layer of doubt I have had about her caring for me. I thought that she must care if she has just lost a night of sleep worrying about me. It never occurred to me that Sue would lose any sleep over what I tell her. I was truly shocked. Tears filled my eyes and I wept silently as we continued to talk.

Sue had always told me that she cared and loved me – as a client and a person. She had done a lot for me but I always wondered if it was just a role for her. For years I believed in her love and caring for me. But as my own demons continued to assault me, I had a much harder time believing that Sue cared about me. I had convinced myself that she wanted me alive just so that she didn't have a "blemish on her record." But when she told me about her sleepless night, I realized that Sue wanted me alive because she wanted me in the world. She really believed that I made a difference and was worth saving.

I was too shocked by this insight to verbalize any of it to Sue while we were talking on the phone. I wasn't sure what to say to her. I apologized for causing her to lose sleep. I promised I wouldn't hurt myself and that she didn't have to lose more sleep worrying about me. After I hung up I realized that I couldn't cause her another sleepless night. No matter how horrendous my pain and despair, I couldn't put her in this position again.

When I saw her after her vacation, I would tell her what a powerful effect her admission had on me. I would promise that I would never again cause her so much worry that she couldn't sleep. I knew this meant that I couldn't think of suicide as an option anymore. I was scared about this because the pain I lived with still was unbearable. Nevertheless, I couldn't be a person who causes someone I love this much grief. I couldn't do it. I didn't know how but I had to find a way to keep the promise I just made to myself. The next time I saw Sue, I would have to find a way of explaining all of this to her.

A dramatic shift

Although the last vignette signaled a change for Elizabeth, the suicidal thoughts and feelings were still very much with us. Some of the urgency had begun to abate, but the intense despair remained. As we continued to address this issue in a variety of ways, a new memory gave Elizabeth a much better understanding of the origin of her suicidal "option." The memory allowed us to understand these thoughts and feelings in a new way, and finally, after many years, we could begin to create a path away from Suicide Is Always an Option. At the same time, relief from the threat of suicide brought in new dilemmas that were in many ways equally difficult.

Elizabeth: A dangerous re-enactment

After spending years struggling with suicidal actions, I finally made sense of a set of behaviors I had carried out many times. This came about after experiencing a flood of new memories last night and explaining their content to Sue.

I remembered the men forcing me to play out a scenario that ensured my silence: Take a knife, put it to my throat and then vow that I would kill myself rather than tell their secrets. I was relieved to tell Sue that acting out this ritual was what I had been doing. It didn't explain away every incident of suicidal thoughts, feelings or actions over the years, but it helped me know that part of why acting out this ritual always felt so strange to me was that I was replaying what I had been taught. The despair and depression I continued to feel were real but the strong urge to take my life was not of my own doing – certainly not in this automatic, choreographed part that I played out over the past several years. I finally had a way of understanding my own behavior.

I was actually excited describing to Sue how last night I had another bout of suicidal thoughts and wanted to go into the kitchen and get a knife. But this time I told myself that this was what the men want, not what I want. This seemed to give me some foundation on which I could make a stand when the suicidal urges began again. After learning this, the urge lessened. I could finally separate despair and depression from the urge to take my life. This knowledge made me very, but not totally, relieved. Maybe I could keep myself safe now despite still living in unbearable pain. We both hoped that this would be the case.

Sue: Destroying the pills

I didn't dare let myself get too excited, but today's session sure felt like a milestone. We had been battling the suicidal impulses for years now and I was weary. They had seemed almost implacable and I had begun to fear that we could never really eradicate them.

But, in our last session, Elizabeth told me she wanted to do a ritual with me and throw away all the pills that had haunted her throughout her struggles against her suicidal demons. I jumped at the chance. So today, she brought in a bag of pills, some prescription and some not. We sat on the sofa, armed with scissors and a wastebasket between us, and cut and ripped, emptying out everything she had brought. It was surprisingly lighthearted. Taking her cue, I joked with her about how to break the seals, how hard the packaging was, what the cleaning service might think on discovering this treasure trove; we generally had fun together until the task was done. It was a tremendous relief to me and I think, to Elizabeth. I also was reminded of the "old Elizabeth": that person I had known in pre-trauma time, who was so fun-loving, sharp-witted, and even light-hearted. Nice to know she was still in there. I would so love to believe that we were done with this chapter, but I didn't dare let myself consider it. I would have to wait and see what happened after today's very cathartic exercise.

Elizabeth: Trapped

I could feel the change in me. I now knew that suicide was no longer an option. I told Sue. She was relieved. I wouldn't cause her any more sleepless nights. I wouldn't continue to worry Ellen about whether I would be alive when she came home from work. I could finally say with certainly that I would not take my own life, but I was not at peace. I was depressed. I still believed – was certain – that I would live the rest of my days in agony. There would be no escape, no hope, no sense of self and no ability to feel peace or deep connection with another. I would try to give Ellen the life she deserves but I would not be able to do it with joy. I couldn't feel contentment, self-fulfillment, happiness or purpose. The truth was, I said to Sue, I still wanted to die. But now I was caught because I promised that I would not die by my own hand. My despair deepened as this trap settled all around me.

I explained my "Catch-22" to Sue. I believed that no one, including Sue, would ever believe how much pain I lived with unless I killed myself. If I didn't kill myself, people would think I was exaggerating the amount of pain I had had and was experiencing. They would think I exaggerated the effects this trauma and torture have had on my life. No one would believe that I couldn't go on and that I had nothing left for the fight unless I actually ended this fight. There was no way to talk about or prove the extent of my agony without the act of suicide. It was the one act that is seen as the ultimate expression of agony, despair and hopelessness. Without suicide no one would ever know the extent or depth of the despair and hopelessness that defined my existence.

Sue strongly disagreed with this. She emphatically stated, "I do believe you. I know your stories. I know how much you have suffered and are suffering. You do not need to kill yourself. I believe you and I have witnessed your agony. And I believe that things can get better. Someday your life can be good."

As I held Sue's hand I wondered about her belief that there was still an "old Elizabeth" left that possessed qualities that I longed to have again, including some sense of peace. Sue told me again that she was convinced that I was not condemned to the kind of life I envision. I wished I held her beliefs.

How does it end?

After Elizabeth realized that her suicidal urges were largely fueled by her torturers' wishes, the power they had over her began to diminish. She was no longer in a constant struggle for her life. However, now knowing the full extent of her trauma, she still found herself in a deep despair. We had to address this in our work together. Finding a way to integrate memories that will never completely disappear into her life story became our shared task. The focus of therapy began to shift from looking past to looking forward. Because Sue believed that our relationship to each other and our ability to relate to each other as people was primary, she chose not to take a "professional stance" that would have prevented her from sharing some of her own personal and deeply held beliefs. To honor our relationship, she willingly read books and articles at Elizabeth's request. Sue also openly and honestly engaged in discussions of values, ethics and spiritual questions. For Elizabeth, these discussions were a vital bridge out of trauma time.

Elizabeth: The need to find meaning

My time with Sue began to have another focus: my own search for meaning. Again, today, this was what I had to discuss. I felt a bit reticent to delve deeply into my search. Sue is a therapist, not a spiritual leader. Still, she had talked with me about the deep purpose music fills in her life and was willing to talk with me about finding meaning for my life in different ways. We had already discussed in some depth what we both struggled with when we were sitting with clients whose lives had been changed by trauma and torture. Today I needed to explore what it meant to no longer be the same person who started this journey many years ago. That person died during the process of uncovering my past. I might not have been strongly suicidal anymore, but I was still left without a clear sense of meaning for my life. Some people can live well without a strong and deep sense of purpose or meaning. That is not true for me. To live a life without meaning is to live in despair. I explained to Sue that while I hadn't been spending countless hours planning my death, I also was not rejoicing that I had made it out of the process alive. I had to begin to rebuild my sense of purpose and meaning for my life so that when these suicidal urges surfaced again, I would have a new foundation on which to fight them. And to use a cliché, I wanted to thrive – not just survive.

But I needed help. Maybe Sue wasn't the person to guide me on this quest. On the other hand, maybe I didn't need a guide but a companion. Today I brought with me Victor Frankl's book *Man's Search for Meaning*. I hoped that Sue would agree to read it. I wanted her to know how important – essential – my own search was. She was open to reading it. I breathed more deeply as I explained my dilemma. Frankl gives some voice to my struggle. I don't agree with everything he says but many things resonate for me.

Sue listened and shared some of her own thoughts on suffering, forgiveness and healing. Our conversation seemed filled with respect and a reverence for these topics. Yes, I would be able to continue to discuss this soul searching with Sue. She was respectful, shared many of my opinions and was nonjudgmental. In the very beginning of working on all these new memories, we discussed using music as a source of spiritual strength. I was grateful to Sue that I could share how music helped keep me sane during my years of abuse. She said, "It saved your soul." She was right. Now I turn to these discussions again. Music, meaning, purpose – if I am to live, I must live with these things infusing my soul once again.

Sue: Reading Frankl – Elizabeth's search for meaning

This week, I read Frankl's book *Man's Search for Meaning*. Elizabeth asked that I read it to help me understand what she is trying to work through. The book was written in 1946, and chronicles Dr. Frankel's story of survival in the concentration camps and how he used his experience in the concentration camp to inform his work as a therapist helping people find meaning in their lives. This was Elizabeth's preoccupation.

She knew that she needed to make meaning out of her "concentration camp" experience to move on, embrace her own life and let go of her suicidal preoccupation. She was reading this book with sharp eyes, looking for clues to help her avoid suicide as the only possible recourse and find something for which to live.

When we met yesterday, we spent most of the session talking about the book and how it impressed us. I had found the book to be powerful in many ways. Though the story itself is not new, it is a grim reminder of the capacities for both evil and good in humankind. It showed in harsh light the way people survive and die in the worst conditions and attempted to delineate why some survived and some didn't. Finding meaning was the key, and it was clear to both of us that Elizabeth was desperate to find that for herself.

The book also hit me hard as I read it, and I imagined Elizabeth seeing herself in the pages. I had spent years imagining her in all kinds of inhuman scenarios, but the universally accepted reality of the concentration camp pictures that came into my mind brought her experience into even sharper focus. She identified herself with people who had been debased to such levels that they barely recognized themselves as humans. This was how she saw herself, and I was again taken aback by her internal picture of herself.

At the same time, I was tremendously relieved to be in conversation again with the scholar I had remembered in pre-trauma time. Here again was the deeply thoughtful person who could navigate complex theological and spiritual dilemmas with ease. She was working out of a less-traumatic place now, and although her trauma was far from disappearing, she could leave it aside enough to consider these ideas. I have always loved these kinds of discussions and left our session stimulated by our conversation. I knew I was the therapist and that this was in the service of Elizabeth finding her own meaning system for survival, but it was also deeply satisfying to have this conversation with her. I felt connected, stimulated and encouraged that we were able to talk in these ways.

CHAPTER 6

THE SHAME FILTER

THE THIRD FACTOR we encountered during trauma time we have labeled "The Shame Filter." It resides on the extreme end of embarrassment and shame. For example, it is a common experience to feel embarrassed when you've done something that is a mistake or foolish or silly. Usually, the feeling dissipates along with the blushed cheeks. Farther down the continuum is shame, which is a different experience. It is an emotion that brings with it painful beliefs that cause people to label themselves as bad, unworthy of love and worthless.

As clinicians we often hear our clients talk about feeling worthless, unlovable or not good enough. As a client talks about experiences that were traumatic, it is common for her not only to recall a memory via senses — sight, sound, smell, touch — but also to recall the emotions attached to the experience. Since many survivors experience shame as a part of an abusive, traumatic event, when that person is retelling or remembering the experience of abuse, she may also experience shame. As her experience includes more traumatic experiences, especially those in which she suffered abuse at the hands of someone she trusted, the survivor often internalizes abusive acts as something she deserved. It can happen that the "true, factual story" becomes that they "deserved what they got" because they are worthless and do not deserve to be treated with respect and care. The urge to make some sense out of abusive experience also contributes to that conclusion: It had to be my fault; otherwise, there is no way to make any sense out of the experience. It is this kind of shame that we define as *the profound and pervasive belief and experience of oneself that s/he has no redeemable value.*

For us, shame was a regular part of our therapy from the beginning. However, in pre-trauma time, we could both recognize the shame, put it into context and then work together on understanding it and lessening its power. Elizabeth had enough sense of herself to be able to balance out some of her worst shame with a reservoir of other recent experiences. She could find at least a little indication of hope or value in her life. We could recover from a misunderstanding that created some shame for Elizabeth and get back to a more stable place in our relationship by using Elizabeth's sense of our relationship and what she know about Sue's beliefs about her. In short, even at its most painful, the shame Elizabeth felt could be understood and countered by our efforts at reconnection.

The Shame Filter versus shame

We found something different was happening between us as we entered trauma time more deeply. The shame that Elizabeth experienced during trauma time seemed tenfold as strong as in pre-trauma time. The depth of her shame made it impossible for Elizabeth to experience herself as having any value or worth at all – even when she was not in the middle of re-experiencing traumatic events. Once trauma time started and as the other trauma time factors took hold, Elizabeth found herself drowning in intense, overwhelming shame that impeded her capacity to reflect on her own strengths, values, history or prior beliefs about herself. As the trauma memories accumulated, the strength of her belief in her worthlessness became more and more ingrained in every exchange between us. She could not reassure herself of her own worth, nor could she count on the history of our relationship to lessen the experience of shame in the moment. Because of the complication of Temporary Is Permanent, we had only our immediate experience, which could be easily distorted by the enormity of shame that Elizabeth was experiencing. It was this overwhelming shame that caused so much distortion in Elizabeth's experiencing the present moment. As we met as co-authors to discuss our experiences in therapy, we came to label this intense distortion that shame caused Elizabeth the Shame Filter.

We define the Shame Filter as *"the persistent and overwhelming experience of shame that resides in the trauma client, not in the therapist, but that affects both client and therapist during trauma time. It serves to distort the client's perspective of the relationship to such an extent that clear communication is virtually impossible."* Although Elizabeth's experience of shame in recalling her traumatic memories was pervasive, the Shame Filter was a different, more intense experience that got between us in ways that we had not experienced together before.

The Shame Filter complicated the normal "process of therapy" in profound ways. Without a Shame Filter, we knew that the client and therapist could go through a "rough spot" in a their relationship and come out the other side with some sense that although it was difficult, it was a shared experience. In that case, both people can "tell the story" of the misunderstanding and feel reconnected as they rebuild their connection. The story may be experienced differently to some extent, but the gist of the misunderstanding is shared between then. In that case, the empathic connection is rebuilt and, it is hoped, the relationship proves itself strong enough to support the challenge. As the Shame Filter appeared and grew in prominence, this normal process of connection-disconnection-reconnection was extremely difficult and often not possible. Of course, Sue made mistakes, wasn't empathic, distanced herself or misunderstood Elizabeth at various times. These things were not the norm but it sometimes felt that way to Elizabeth because the Shame Filter amplified and/or distorted these mistakes. The Shame Filter caused Elizabeth to believe that Sue was doing these things because Sue knew that Elizabeth was worthless or that she hated her.

The Shame Filter meant that we often did not come even close to sharing each other's perceptions of what was going on and were at a loss to explain the disconnect. We could no longer jointly assess what was working and not working between us. We could no longer trust our own perceptions. We became more and more distant even though we were both trying as hard as we could to keep our connection. We believed that this distance further contributed to the Shame Filter as our capacity to feel empathically connected to each other diminished in a kind of vicious circle. We were often confused, frustrated, hurt and angry.

While the Shame Filter resided in Elizabeth, it certainly had a significant impact on Sue. When Elizabeth expressed shame in pre-trauma time, Sue was used to Elizabeth giving her clear feedback that accurately reflected the experience between them. Even when there was disagreement or when Sue had inadvertently done something that hurt Elizabeth, Elizabeth was able to talk through these experiences, correct misunderstandings and feel closer to Sue as a result of our discussions. This changed in trauma time when the Shame Filter became established.

The Shame Filter was perhaps the most difficult aspect of our therapy to fully understand. It constantly surprised both of us with its power, tenancy and destructiveness. It was easy to miss it entirely and carry on in the belief that we were understanding each other, only to find, moments later, that our communication had been hijacked by the Shame Filter and we were nowhere near understanding each other. It often left us feeling hurt, misunderstood or shamed without quite knowing why. We understood in retrospect that sometimes we would lash out at each other rather than experience the intensity of the shame in the room. We searched for concrete reasons, usually finding very little substance. The Shame Filter was a formidable enemy, and we don't think we can underscore this enough. Both of us have heard clinicians talk in exasperated tones of clients who are "manipulative, demanding, inconsistent, irrational and accusatory." While there certainly are other explanations possible, we believe that these clinicians are also likely to be sitting with someone in trauma time who is desperately trying to navigate through a Shame Filter that prohibits any clear view of what is really happening between client and therapist. The Shame Filter distorts everything and needs to be understood and acknowledged before more meaningful interchanges can take place.

Once the Shame Filter was in place, Elizabeth accused Sue of doing or saying things that shamed her. Sue did not believe she was doing anything to purposely shame Elizabeth, but Elizabeth's feedback during these times was consistent – Sue was shaming her. As careful and genuine as Sue's empathic statements usually were, and as much as she truly cared for Elizabeth, nothing could get through the Shame

Filter untouched. If Sue offered help, Elizabeth heard it as a statement of blame. A statement of care and concern was doubted. Sue's vacations became an indication of Sue's disgust at being with Elizabeth. Over time, this kind of feedback from Elizabeth caused Sue to become less responsive and hesitant to provide feedback or empathic comments. At times Sue found herself withdrawing from Elizabeth and when trauma time and the Shame Filter were at their worst, she questioned her skills as a therapist and felt her own shame at not being able to help ease Elizabeth's pain.

This chapter shows the effects of the Shame Filter on our relationship and on us as individuals. The vignettes in the chapter illustrate the progression of Elizabeth's experience of shame that became the Shame Filter, and then the lessening of the Shame Filter after new memories stopped. At the very beginning of new memories, Elizabeth had some capacity to trust her relationship with Sue to help her tell shameful memories. However, as trauma time continued, this quickly changed and Elizabeth experienced more and more difficulty believing Sue could see her as something other than disgusting, useless and worthless. As trauma time wore on, the Shame Filter became more consistent and was complicated by Sue's shame that had been triggered by the Shame Filter. There are also vignettes that show the activities that lessened the Shame Filter enough to allow us to feel enough of a connection to continue therapy. Thankfully, as new memories stopped, the Shame Filter faded and we were able to begin to regroup and begin to experience each other in ways that were nurturing and affirming.

Shame intensifies

As soon as trauma time started, intense shame was a part of most interactions between us. However, initially there were things that Sue could do or say that allowed Elizabeth to combat the shame and push through it so that Sue could be with her in the experience and help her sort through what the new memories meant for her. The following vignettes give a picture of what shame look like in early trauma time before the Shame Filter was firmly in place, what Sue did that allowed Elizabeth to feel her acceptance and how Elizabeth was able to take in this acceptance and continue to maintain a connection to Sue despite the shame she was experiencing.

Elizabeth: Naked child running

I had told Sue that I thought I remembered everything that happened to me as a child. I had no idea that there was more abuse to remember. I was tentative with Sue today and watched for her reactions to the images I presented to her. My imagination is very active and it's very easy for me to talk about my internal landscape and internal struggles using images. I know that not everyone can separate an active imagination from some pathological process. I didn't know which side of the equation Sue would be on. I didn't want her to think that I have several personalities inside of me. I took the risk and told Sue about a particular image that had haunted me for at least a week now.

Shaking, I closed my eyes and began to describe a small child trapped in a cave. I hesitated and expressed the fear I felt as this image unfolded. Sue asked me if I wanted to hold her hand as I described the scene. I thought she meant she would hold my hand in the image, so I said, "Yes." Sue moved her chair closer to mine and took my hand. That surprised me but I was very comforted by it and found the courage to complete the picture I saw in my mind. It was of me as a terrified child – naked, alone, without any resources – trapped in a cold cave. The child was curled up with her back to the cave wall. She had a gun to her head. She told me, "This is the only way out." I didn't know what the image meant, but I knew it captured the feeling of sheer terror and a desire for death that has been with me since new memories of abuse surfaced.

Sue was concerned that the girl looked like she was planning to kill herself. Sue asked the girl why she was holding the gun to her head. I told her that the girl believed the only escape was her death. Sue gently talked to her. She reassured the girl that she was safe now and didn't need to use the gun. Sue asked me to try to negotiate with the girl. The girl was too terrified to give Sue or me the gun, but she agreed to put the gun down next to her on the ground.

Once the girl put down the gun, Sue asked what this child needed and I told Sue she needed a blanket. We visualized giving the girl a blanket. For now, that was all this girl could accept. Her terror was deep and trust was too dangerous. I knew that this girl would continue to be with me. I'm glad that Sue accepted her and felt comfortable sharing my inner world of images. Sue wanted to help me in whatever way allowed me to voice my experience. She was comfortable talking with me to name and visualize my desire to die by my own hand in such a deep and vulnerable way. Sue's acceptance helped me move through the shame I felt and allowed me to tell her about the image and what it represented. I didn't have to experience it alone anymore.

Sue: Holding hands

It felt like we were in a new place today, and the stories that Elizabeth was remembering seemed to be new to her. Until now, she'd been letting me know the history that she had worked on in her prior therapy. Today was different, and I could see just how difficult it was to put a narrative on this new picture. She was deep in a metaphor, and the image was that of a child who was completely alone. I offered her my hand and she came out of her fog enough to look a bit surprised but then grateful. She reached out; I pulled my chair close enough, and spent the rest of the session holding her hand as she told her story. It was clear that the physical contact helped ease the shame and isolation of the story and of the retelling of it.

Elizabeth: Telling Sue about Sarah

I couldn't remember if I'd ever told anyone about Sarah. Many people knew how important my first guitar was to me but I'd never told anyone that I'd named it. I really wanted to tell Sue about Sarah and tell her that her name means "goodness." I usually am embarrassed about naming an inanimate object. But I'd been feeling so much shame lately and felt it important that Sue knew this guitar helped me to remain connected to my soul when all of these horrific things were happening to me. I was a little worried that she wouldn't understand but got over my shame when I remembered how connected Sue is to music. If anyone could understand how a guitar helped to save me and shield me from shame it would be Sue.

When I told her about Sarah, she got a big grin on her face and wanted to know more. It was still hard for me to talk about. I guess a lot of people name objects and have strong attachments to them. This felt so different to me, partly because it was during a time I learned to feel so much shame for just being alive. I felt ashamed that I had to rely on a guitar to allow me to find a voice and sing my pain. Sue reassured me that there was nothing for me to feel ashamed about. In the end, I'm glad I fought through my strong shame to tell her about the precious thing I own. My guitar that helped save me by giving voice to my pain, anguish and shame. My guitar that allowed me the only way to express out loud the crippling pain I lived with. It was like sharing a part of my soul with Sue. And, thank God, she understood.

Getting harder as the Shame Filter becomes established

As trauma time continued, Elizabeth's memories became more traumatic and intense, and our relationship was threatened even more as the Shame Filter grew. Elizabeth often told Sue that she was "drowning in shame" and began to react increasingly negatively to Sue, regardless of whether there had been a therapeutic error on her part.

The Shame Filter generated a lot of anger in Elizabeth, especially at herself. However, this anger also greatly affected Sue. Innocent questions from Sue could be met with a very angrily charged answer. At these times, Elizabeth was in so much pain that she did not have the wherewithal to explain the cause or target of her anger. Other times, Elizabeth was furious at Sue because she believed Sue was purposely trying to shame her. As we delved deeper into Elizabeth's memories, it became clearer that some of the intensity of the dynamic between us was complicated by particular experiences Elizabeth endured that were designed to induce shame in its victims. These experiences happened in "the circle of shame" that Elizabeth described in her autobiography.

When the Shame Filter was at its worst, Elizabeth was in the midst of re-experiencing what it was like to kneel in the "circle of shame."

We found that even a question from Sue asking Elizabeth what she needed was a trigger for her experience when words were twisted and meanings horribly manipulated. Because the men had sadistically asked what Elizabeth wanted or needed in the circle, Sue's questions when Elizabeth was most vulnerable easily triggered a re-experiencing of the circle of shame with Sue cast as the perpetrator. Even though Elizabeth always knew that Sue was not one of the men, under the distortions of the Shame Filter and the power of this memory, she easily fell into attributing to Sue the same motives as the men in the basement.

Although Elizabeth had explained the circle of shame to Sue, neither of us realized how much it directly affected our interactions until we were discussing writing this book. During our therapy, the circle of shame and the Shame Filter caused massive confusion for both of us as Elizabeth continued to experience overwhelming levels of self-hatred and shame, and at its worst, attributed shaming motives to Sue. Sue's experience during this time reflected an enormous amount of confusion because her best efforts of being empathic and helpful triggered horrific shame in Elizabeth.

Sue became aware that Elizabeth was very tuned into Sue's behavior and expected Sue to react negatively to her. During our therapy together we did not explain this phenomenon as "the Shame Filter." But Sue knew that it became extremely important for her to acknowledge and label anything she knew might contribute to the confusion and shame Elizabeth was feeling. Although this certainly meant being aware of what was going on in the relationship in the moment, it also required that Sue be highly aware of her own internal experience. If she was tired, distracted by other life situations that made her less than 100 percent present, there was a high possibility that Elizabeth would think Sue was shaming her.

The following vignettes highlight how the Shame Filter significantly changed or distorted how Elizabeth experienced her relationship with

Sue. The first three vignettes show how much Elizabeth struggled with the Shame Filter's grip on her ability to trust Sue's acceptance and care for her. The last vignette is an example of acknowledging the importance of authenticity in battling the Shame Filter.

Sue: Cold and distant

Today I felt awful. I had one of those drippy, sneezy head colds that kept me close to the Kleenex box at all times. For some time now, during sessions, I had been pulling my chair closer to Elizabeth's and holding her hand. She felt that it helped her feel less like she was "on display" and more like I was really with her as she told her story. Today, without giving it too much thought, I kept my chair at a distance and armed myself with a Kleenex box. I couldn't imagine anyone wanting me closer than at least eight feet! I thought it would be pretty obvious why I had kept my distance, and at one level it was. But Elizabeth's reaction was immediate and powerful. The new distance between us, however she intellectually understood it, meant only one thing: I had abandoned her, like everyone else. She had misplaced her trust in me. Finally, her worst fears were confirmed: Once I heard her stories, I would become disgusted with her and want to move away.

I was horrified that she had taken that meaning from my only partially aware behavior. It was the last thing I wanted to convey. It was incredibly hard for her to acknowledge the shame my actions stirred up in her. Part of her knew so absolutely that my action was completely understandable, and even gracious. However, the act of physically moving away and refusing touch was just too powerful a message for her to override. At the end of the session, she became quiet and asked: "When will I be normal?" We talked about it for some time, but I wasn't convinced at all that she felt any better when she left the session.

Elizabeth: Telling a short story takes 50 minutes

I was furious with myself. Goddamn it. No matter how hard I tried, no matter how much I wanted to talk to Sue, no matter how desperate I felt, once I got into her office I could hardly get the words out. I felt so humiliated by the things I'd been remembering. More shame and guilt and fucking slime. Covered in it. All the time.

I got into Sue's office and I shut down. I wanted to talk, but I was afraid. I felt so ashamed by the details I had to describe. Who wants to tell someone about being raped and, even worse, being forced to do things that are so humiliating? It took me over an hour to get out one small memory. And today wasn't the first time this has happened. It was getting worse and worse and worse. I was so angry with myself. I hardly got to spend any time with Sue as it was, then when I was actually with her, I couldn't say a fucking word. I sat there like a deaf mute. I was unable to respond to anything she said. She asked if I could hear her. I wasn't able to form the words that would allow me to not be so alone in all of this. She was the only one I could share these memories with. They are so horrendous. I didn't want anyone else to know about them. Even though Sue said that it's not my fault and that she still loved me, I could get only one or two words out at a time. Why was I such a fucking loser?

Elizabeth: End of session suddenly felt shaming

It was time to go because the clock said so. I knew Sue had another client coming in a little while. I had things to do. Despite my knowing this, when session ended and it was clear that Sue wanted me to leave, I was overcome with shame. I felt like the only reason she wanted me to go was because I was disgusting and that she couldn't stand to be with me anymore. I felt devastated. I felt so ashamed for being me. I knew it was just time to go, but the feeling was so strong and powerful. This had happened at the end of a session for a few weeks. And it seemed to be getting worse.

Sue: Telling it like it is

I have always tried to keep my personal life out of the therapy room when I can. If I'm sick, my clients are informed, and if there is a family emergency, there are times when some information is shared. Today I took a risk with Elizabeth that stepped a bit outside my comfort zone. I had to tell her about Jan, a friend from high school who has cancer.

She was staying in my home and receiving special treatment at a nearby hospital. I was her caregiver, and I was on duty when I was not away at my office. I was watching her die and it was very painful. Half of my brain was with Jan, even when I made my very best effort to stay present with my clients. I knew that Elizabeth could tell, so I needed to let her know that any "abandonment" in the air was about Jan, not her. I told her the basics of the situation and that I was doing everything I could to be present with her, but that if she felt me "leave," it had more to do with my friend than it did her. I asked her to let me know if she felt my absence and I would let her know where I had "gone." I was pretty sure she was relieved, but I knew for sure that I was.

The Shame Filter at its worst

As the Shame Filter "thickened" over time, the relationship we have been saying is so central to our therapy was severely challenged. We were fully in the muck. Once Elizabeth's memories began to include experiences of torture, the Shame Filter threatened to cause her to end our therapeutic relationship. Elizabeth could not feel any connection with Sue and did not experience her as helpful or caring. Sue felt this disconnection and could not find anything to do or say that could lessen the effects of the Shame Filter. It also sometimes caused Sue to become more distant since she was not feeling effective as a therapist and worried about saying or doing something that would increase Elizabeth's anger and shame. During this time almost nothing Sue said could help, and Elizabeth was so overpowered by a deep sense of shame that she truly believed that Sue hated her and found her disgusting.

Writing and sharing these vignettes was especially painful for both of us. We shared feelings, horrified that we were being portrayed by the other in such negative ways, and repeatedly asked each other "Was it really that bad?" In many ways it was, although obviously we persevered.

These vignettes highlight what was a very confusing and painful time between us. They describe some of the worst experiences we had. Because of the Shame Filter, the experiences we had of each other were very distorted and did not allow for any kind of shared reality between us. At that point in our time together, it was almost impossible for Elizabeth to see anything at all positive about Sue and her exchanges with Elizabeth. One of the most painful experiences between us centered on a very angry letter that Elizabeth had given to Sue explaining how disappointed, angry and frustrated she was with Sue's inability to help her. She questioned Sue's abilities and motives as a therapist. This letter and Sue's reaction became the focus of months of work between us as we worked through the hurt and implications for both of us as individuals and for our working relationship. These vignettes show how the Shame Filter made it impossible for us to communicate or have a shared reality or one another. The last vignette speaks to how much the Shame Filter affected Sue as well and how she managed those feelings.

Sue: Twilight Zone

We had been in the midst of rolling memories – each one more horrific than the last – for some time and we were both exhausted. Today was yet another new memory: this one in "the basement," with multiple perpetrators intent on humiliating their child victims. I knew how hard this story was to tell and it took Elizabeth a good part of the session to get the main points out. I did my best to listen and be available and empathic and tried to stay with her in the telling and re-living of these memories. I was conscious of not being distracted; I was not disgusted by her having had that experience, nor was I "leaving" the room to avoid the pain. I felt connected to her. However, somewhere near the end of the session, she became silent and then was enraged at me for not "getting it." She was convinced I had emotionally abandoned her and was judging her harshly for her "role" in the scene.

I tried my best to understand what I had said, or failed to say, that had sent her into such despair, but was totally unable to do so. She was convinced I was shaming her and had been "just waiting" to abandon her. Any references to our years of history and years of recovering together were spurned. Any empathic statements were equally discounted. They meant nothing and to even bring them up seemed to add more shame to the mix. We talked for 15 minutes and got absolutely nowhere. It was like we were suddenly in a new relationship. I felt like I was in the Twilight Zone, with no reality that I could count on. I ended up feeling completely helpless and a bit ashamed of my own inability to be able to figure out what was going on enough to offer the words that would reach her. I had some faith that we would figure this out eventually, but history said that it might be weeks or months before we could understand what happened today with any clarity at all. Meanwhile, I was flying blind.

Elizabeth: Why can't Sue help me? Why is she shaming me?

I just didn't get it. What did Sue get out of shaming me? What did she get out of making me feel covered in slime just like the men did? Why couldn't she help me? It was her job. It was her job to help me say things that I'd been choking on. She could see I was struggling. Why didn't she help? She asked me what I needed. Well, if I knew what the fuck I needed, I would have told tell her! It made me feel even more ashamed than I was already feeling. Why didn't she understand how shaming that question is? She asked it over and over. I was so angry with her. I felt intense shame because I was feeling like a non-human – like an alien covered in slime – and Sue was saying that she saw something different. Well, big fucking deal. I couldn't see it or feel it. It just made me feel worse. Sometimes I hated her because she made me feel so ashamed at all of things I can't think or do or feel. It was hopeless. I tried explaining how a client-centered therapist would respond to me and she got very defensive. She thought she was doing everything that I explained to her but she wasn't. And I felt too confused to be able to give her a lecture on client-centered therapy. I tried and it got me nowhere.

Left with no words: Sue

Today was such a rough session with Elizabeth. She told yet another horrific memory in halting tones and I tried to use all my best skills to find a way of empathically resonating with her. I tried to put myself in her experience, to know what it was like to be so abused and humiliated, to have no control of my body or my destiny. I could get only a small inkling of what that level of shame might feel like. It felt demoralizing and exhausting, and the sense of helplessness that she experienced left me with no words that could begin to reflect her experience. The horror, pain and humiliation were overwhelming, and my usual tools of verbalizing, symbolizing or reflecting back to Elizabeth were not accessible. Everything I could imagine saying felt inadequate and discounting. As a result, I was quiet for much of the storytelling, trying to just use non-verbal communications to let her know I was with her. Unfortunately, to her, my silence felt like an indictment, and she was hurt and angry when I didn't immediately respond. She told me it was proof that I saw her as "a throw-away person" and didn't care at all – the very impression I didn't want to give! I tried to find the words she needed, but by then the damage was done and she left feeling hurt and probably abandoned.

Elizabeth: Not being able to play "Mother, Mother"

I just couldn't believe this. It happened again. I brought in Cris Williamson's song "Mother, Mother" to play for Sue. That song hits me so deeply. It hits my grief and speaks so poignantly to my mother's betrayal: "Mother, mother keep me safe from harm. Hold me in your arms and don't forget me." It breaks my heart. I thought if I could play it for Sue, she would see how deeply my heart has been broken by all of my mother's betrayals. But this is the second time I've tried to play it for her. I lugged in the CD player and put in the CD. I couldn't get the words out to even explain what the song was or why it was so important to me or why it was so difficult to play. So I sat there like an idiot. I couldn't get anything out of my mouth, and Sue started saying ridiculous shit. I just didn't get it. The more she talked, the more furious I became. Why couldn't she be with me when I was in such agony? This hurt so much. The pain crushed me and she was looking bored or annoyed.

So I did it again. I stormed out. I just couldn't sit there and be ridiculed anymore. I already knew what a piece of shit I was. I already knew I wasn't good enough for my mother to want to protect me. She forgot about me over and over again. That's all I wanted Sue to know. But she forgot about me too. It was too much. I couldn't risk letting her see me so crushed, not when she was clearly not interested in how much agony I was in.

Sue's shock at the letter

The letter from hell! I'd never felt this bad about myself as a therapist. I received a nine-page letter from Elizabeth that went into great detail about all my failings as a therapist for her. In it she accused me of not listening to her, telling her what to do, imposing my own agenda on her, not understanding her experience at all, being unempathic, using theory to distance our relationship, telling her how she feels and pretty much failing her in every way. There was little in it to reassure me that we had any hope of continuing and, in fact, her first paragraph indicated that this might be the end of our therapy together.

While I pride myself in being able to take in criticism and not get too defensive, this went so far beyond that. I was speechless. I couldn't find a foothold to anchor any of this. It did not compute. It was a blanket indictment of everything I'd said and done for 10 years with Elizabeth. I hadn't a clue how to proceed. It would take a very long time to respond to each of these accusations and the enormity of the shame imbedded in all those pages. I didn't know where to start and I felt awful. I had no energy left, and this was a battle that would demand every ounce of strength I could muster. I couldn't call her. The shame, hurt, anger, confusion and helplessness were overwhelming.

Elizabeth's shock at Sue's reaction

I was so fed up with Sue that I gave her the letter I wrote last night. I decided I needed to be honest with her and let her know how frustrated I was with her and her actions. I didn't know what else to do. I'd told her many times to stay with my experience rather than try to sugarcoat things. But she didn't listen to me. I didn't care if I looked like I was ok. If I told you I was in agony, you should have believed me! Why couldn't she do that? I'd just had it. I needed her to know how bad things are between us. I didn't want to attack her but I did want her to know how frustrated, humiliated and angry I was.

She was shocked by the letter. She could hardly say anything. I was shocked that she didn't know I felt this way. I'd told her all of these things before. Why did she feel so hurt? Why was it a surprise? I didn't get it. Hadn't she been listening? Couldn't she see how terrible I felt when she couldn't stay with my experience? Didn't she know how alone I felt when she just sat there and didn't say anything to let me know she understood and heard me? Why couldn't she understand these things? Why was she so upset? If she had been listening to me all this time, this letter should not have been that much of a surprise. Maybe it was time to stop seeing her. I had no idea what else to do.

Sue reaches out to her consultation group

Thank goodness for these women. After reading the letter from Elizabeth, I went to peer consultation today a total basket case, with more than a small amount of my brain convinced that I needed to leave the profession. I felt like I had failed miserably in my ability to help Elizabeth and now, having read her letter, felt it in black and white. I had come to trust these women and we had seen each other through more than a handful of difficult experiences. It had been a place to show our less-than-perfect therapist selves. Well, that's what I did today. I told them as much as I could bear to say of the letter from Elizabeth. I told them my doubts about my own skills and wondered aloud to them if I should quit, refer Elizabeth to someone more competent or what! They were terrific. They asked lots of questions and managed to at least keep me from hanging up my license. They helped me become aware of how much of the trauma that was Elizabeth's had invaded our relationship and how deeply we were imbedded in feeling the shame. I had a good cry, too, and that helped. This therapy with Elizabeth was so exhausting and, at that moment, so completely unrewarding.

Shame Filter compounded by Sue's reaction to the Shame Filter

As trauma time continued and the Shame Filter continued to distort Elizabeth's experience of Sue, Sue began to experience her own shame at being unable to ease Elizabeth's burden by providing any relief or help. At times this caused Sue to question her abilities as a therapist even beyond the overwhelming indictment of Elizabeth's letter. There were a few occasions when Sue experienced guilt for her life circumstances because Elizabeth's life would have taken some similar pathways if those pathways hadn't been disrupted by her trauma. Sometimes Sue had to distance herself from Elizabeth when Elizabeth was particularly insistent that Sue was not being helpful. When Sue felt ashamed at her capacity to help, and found herself feeling like a "perpetrator," she felt an urgency to counter that by fixing the problem. Even though Elizabeth never accused or experienced Sue as a "perpetrator," Sue's own shame fueled this feeling when Elizabeth would express anger or disappointment to Sue. When empathic statements were interpreted as shaming, it was hard to find any place of comfort. At times this led to a spiral of disconnection between us.

The following vignettes illustrate the ways in which Sue worked with the experience of her own shame and tried to minimize the disconnection they caused between us.

Sue: Shame at failure to help

I was feeling so discouraged. Once again, Elizabeth left the session today after letting me know I hadn't helped at all. She railed against my clinical orientation, despaired at my lack of understanding and let me know how little therapy was helping. I so wanted to offer her something, to lessen her shame, shield her from her terror, but everything I tried failed. I was trying to remember that my training told me things often get worse before they get better, but I'm not sure they were supposed to get this bad! Sometimes I'd been able to see her anger and disappointment as a part of her trauma re-experience, but today it felt very personal. In the past, Elizabeth had been able to have moments when she could step back and talk about our relationship in a way that validated what we were doing, but I hadn't heard that for a while. The only "proof" I had that this has any value was her attendance twice a week. Not a lot.

With nothing coming from her that was positive, I was starting to doubt my own capacities. I thought I was being empathic, supportive and present, and I knew I was working really hard, but was beginning to doubt my own perceptions. Maybe I needed some new and different consultation help, although I was ashamed of the way things felt right now and my inability to figure this out. None of the books ever have examples that look like our therapy! Maybe I really couldn't be helpful to her at all. Maybe she was right!

Sue: Shame at "fixer parts"

I had been feeling like such a bad guy in sessions these days that I was starved for a "good moment" that could help me feel some hope again. I knew we were both working hard and neither of us was enjoying this distance, but it was pretty hard to sit with. I felt increasingly desperate and increasingly inept. As a result I wanted to prove to myself that I could do something! I'd worked hard as a therapist to avoid the "fixer" part of me that would like to do the superwoman thing, swooping down with the answer and curing the world of its problems. I do know better. But today, I almost whined at Elizabeth to see if I could convince her of her worth. Of course, it didn't work and I felt worse than before. It wasn't helpful and probably further convinced Elizabeth of my ineptitude. I'm just so frustrated at feeling so completely helpless.

Sue: Shame at own blessings

Well, today, on top of feeling like I wasn't helping very much, I felt like Elizabeth was mad at me for what I have. At this point, I couldn't argue with her, and I felt ashamed of my good fortune. I knew I was the target because I was so connected with her experience, but it was uncomfortable to feel her compare my life to hers and to "win." We were alike in so many ways: our values, politics, interests and ways of being in the world. Although I have tried not to divulge too much of my personal life, she knows I have family and friends, take vacations, have a well-established place in the therapist community and have financial stability.

Although Elizabeth had a long-term relationship, friends and a great deal of professional success, she always measured herself as coming up short. What didn't figure into the equation was the grief over what could have been if her trauma hadn't interrupted her path in so many ways. Beyond the "resume" of what I had and what she didn't have was the experience of the trauma itself. How could I not in some way be apologetic for having had a life relatively free from any trauma and learn of her life that had been so completely formed out of reaction to her trauma? It only made it harder for Elizabeth to talk of her longings and her sense of profound injustice at what she had been denied and I had been granted.

I guessed that to her I looked like the example of what she "could have been." I felt a kind of survivor's guilt – shame at my good fortune – without any way of explaining to either one of us the "why" that we both knew wasn't there. It made me feel uncomfortable about taking those vacations she hated!

Oasis in the storm

As powerful as the Shame Filter was, there were moments when we could take a step back from the chaos of the Shame Filter. At those times, we worked hard to understand it and tried to find ways of combating it. These were moments of connection and hope. We talked often about finding these moments and devised a variety of ways of being with each other that we thought would be helpful. We had moments of looking back on a completely confusing experience with some understanding that would inform how we moved forward. Unfortunately, no plan or shared understanding was immune to the power of the Shame Filter. We might be successful for a time, but the inconsistent nature of the Shame Filter could undo our good intentions easily. Despite these challenges, Elizabeth continued to be creative in the ways she tried to remain connected to Sue. As her memories revealed more brutal forms of torture, Elizabeth became less able to verbally communicate these experiences to Sue.

The following vignettes illustrate three activities Elizabeth initiated with Sue to allow us to feel some connection without using words. These activities allowed us to work around the Shame Filter enough for Elizabeth to be able to continue in therapy and to have hope that she could remain connected to Sue enough to be able to continue to share her unfolding life story.

Long before Elizabeth gave Sue the letter that told Sue how furious and frustrated and disappointed she was with her, Elizabeth wrote Sue many letters in which she was able to tell Sue stories of abuse and how these experiences affected her. Reading a children's book provided a way to recover from a difficult session and be soothed without any risk of distortions from the Shame Filter. Coloring allowed us to share in an activity that was playful, mutual and safe, with no interpretation or conclusions drawn.

Elizabeth: Couldn't talk about memories so wrote Sue a letter

For a few months I'd been writing letters to Sue to describe the new memories I'd been having. In this way, Sue "heard" the most horrendous parts of my experience. The memories from the past few months have been both brutal to remember and brutal to have to share. How could someone torture me and my sister and other children the way they did? How could they force us to watch others being humiliated and raped? I hadn't been able to speak any of these details to Sue. I'd been writing them. Same for today. I got myself to her office knowing that I had another letter to give her with yet another terrible memory of torture and abuse. It took longer for me to give her the letter today than it usually did. Sue extended her hand but I couldn't give her the letter. She reassured me that we could handle whatever was in it. After about half an hour I was able to give Sue the letter. She read it as I sat and worried that she would find me disgusting when she read what had happened. I worried that she would finally tell me to leave her office and never come back because she finally understood what I was.

So far, Sue had never told me to leave her office. She never showed the slightest bit of disgust towards me. But the shame and humiliation I felt still wreaked havoc on my attempts to remain connected to her throughout the retelling of my life's story. After reading the letter, Sue had the dubious task of deciding how to comment on the contents. What do you say to someone who has just told you about being tortured? How do you offer hope to someone who is broken? How do you offer words of comfort to someone who is too numb and deaf with shame to hear anything outside of the inner wall of shame?

However, today, by some true miracle, I was able to hear Sue's support even as I was drowning in my flashbacks and shame. I could hear Sue's words of empathy. I could see that she was not running away. Feeling that connection, however, didn't stop the messages in my head. I asked why Sue supported me, Why didn't she demand that I leave? Why didn't Sue call me a whore? Why didn't she tell me I deserved everything that happened? Why didn't she hate me? I had been trapped in these messages so many times that it was hard to understand this shift to feeling Sue's connection to me. Despite all these old messages, I was able to see just for a little that Sue cared and I was glad I could give her another letter with more of the life story I wish I could rewrite.

Sue: Counteracting the Shame Filter through reading Winnie the Pooh

I'm so glad Elizabeth brought in *Winnie the Pooh*. There was just no other way of being together today. It was clear that Elizabeth was very agitated and uncomfortable but struggled unsuccessfully to articulate it. She did say she wasn't feeling safe and not sure at all that I would "get it." We skirted around another conversation that we both feared would get us nowhere. I knew I probably couldn't reach her in any way that would not be experienced as demeaning or shaming, and she pretty much agreed that there wasn't anything I could say. We both fell on reading together as a way out. I love this book, so it was comforting and familiar to me. Elizabeth loves it too and sat close to me on the sofa as I read it to her. Somehow, we were calmed by words that didn't belong to either of us but were known and trusted by both of us. There was safety in the experience and no risk of shame for either one of us.

Elizabeth: Counteracting the Shame Filter through coloring

I'd been coloring at night for a few months. It was very soothing and helped me get to sleep. A few weeks earlier I decided to bring in some crayons and a coloring book so that Sue and I could color together. It became a very effective way for us to connect – even on the days when I felt the most covered in shame and slime. Those were the days when I most needed to color.

At first I was very tentative with Sue about how to color. I would pick a color and then she would pick a color and we would alternate completing a picture. Now I could ask her to do more things like color left-handed or with our eyes closed. Sometimes I asked her to pick out all of the colors and sometimes I gave her the crayon I wanted her to use. When we colored, I didn't feel the shame. When I asked Sue to do weird things like color with her eyes closed and I could see that she was having a good time, I knew that she wasn't judging me. It was an experience in the here-and-now that enabled me to know she wasn't judging me for the colors I picked or for how I wanted to color. I hadn't experienced that with her for a while, since I was so convinced most of the time that Sue was judging me and that I deserved to be judged because I was such a disgusting person. When we colored, those feelings subsided. I struggled to trust that Sue wouldn't judge me, but once we got going, I had a concrete experience of a nonjudgmental, fun person who cradled me in acceptance.

Reconnecting as the Shame Filter began to fade

Like the other main components of our trauma time experience, the Shame Filter lessened considerably once the memories stopped. The interactions between us began to feel familiar again and we were able to talk without worrying about frustration, anger and misunderstandings derailing our sessions. We had moments when we could look back on recent experiences and see just how much misunderstanding and confusion the Shame Filter had caused, though we weren't using that phrase at the time. We began reconstructing our relationship to regain what we both knew was once there – a strong connection based on shared values and beliefs and years of history together. However, it would be misleading to say this was easy. This was no simple task and took a lot of time and risk for both of us because we had spent a few years drowning in the effects of the Shame Filter and the other factors that made up trauma time. However, we were able to process much of what had happened in retrospect and work to build on those experiences. It was an eye-opening experience for both of us to begin to recognize the distortions that had occurred despite our combined best efforts. The following vignettes illustrate the sense of relief we both felt to be able to relax with each other again and know that our deep connection was still intact.

Sue: Sigh of relief...that felt good

What would have been a potentially huge blow-up and massive hurt turned into something quite manageable, even though it was hurtful. Elizabeth had been telling me about XM radio, the Internet radio station that she thought I might be interested in. She brought in a card today with information on it about how to sign up. She handed me the card when she first came in the room without explaining what it was. I took it and with a dismissive smile threw it in the wastebasket, thinking she had picked up a loose card from one of the magazines in the waiting room.

She immediately looked crushed by my action and was speechless for a few minutes. My heart sank as I realized I had done something awful, but I didn't have a clue about what it was. The miracle was that we started talking about it and I quickly realized my error, retrieved the card and then talked about it with Elizabeth. I explained what I thought it was and why I had tossed it so quickly, and she was able to understand my actions and not take it personally. We were even able to smile about the misunderstanding! While we had been here before, we haven't seen this level of clarity in our conversations for a long time. A misunderstanding occurred. I hurt her feelings. We were able to untangle it and were able to come out on the other side understanding each other without assigned evil motives. Amazing. I was so relieved.

Elizabeth: Finally, I could laugh again

Final-a-ly. I actually laughed when I was with Sue today. We joked around a bit. It felt like old times before all of these memories buried me. Well, maybe not exactly like old times, but it was good to not feel covered in slime and worried about what Sue would think of me once I told her what I had been experiencing. I told her about a funny interaction I had had with my sister the day before and we were able to laugh together.

Maybe things had started to change between us. We talked about how I'd been able to call Sue last week when I needed to talk. I didn't feel the amount of shame I had felt with her for so long. I didn't know if I would ever be able to feel differently. I thought Sue appreciated the lightness between us. I know I did. I didn't know if this was something that would continue. Maybe it was a good sign that I also could talk with her on the phone and not feel like some kind of circus animal being commanded to perform. Maybe I'd turned a corner. I didn't seem to be reactive when Sue said something I didn't agree with. I had more patience with her as we tried to work out something between us. I guess that said something. I just hoped that I didn't go into a hole again. It was so much better when I felt that Sue was in my corner.

Sue: Check ins again

I had so hoped that the suicidal thoughts and feelings had abated. It was hard to hear Ellzabeth talk today of struggling with those same feelings and hear her concern that she couldn't keep herself safe. We talked for a while about what had triggered the feelings again, and her total frustration that they were there at all. She was exhausted by the battle and felt more and more hopeless about getting past these thoughts. Last time, when I offered check-in calls as a way of helping her manage this experience, I ended up injuring her. She was angry and ashamed. She felt infantilized where once she had felt supported. Things had been a little better between us recently, so I took a chance and made that offer again, fully expecting that there was a good chance she would be angry with me for suggesting it. Surprisingly, she was not. She looked relieved and said that it would help her. We set up times to check in on the days between then and her next appointment. I had no idea what shifted that allowed her to take my help, but I was relieved. This will help her get through the next few days and will also help restore the parts of our relationship that have felt so unreachable. Whew.

CHAPTER 7

SAFETY VERSUS TRUST

From safety and trust to despair, and back again

OUR FINAL MAIN factor in many ways encompasses the first three. All the work that is done between the therapist and client is in some way dependent on the level of safety and trust in the relationship. The level of safety and trust achieved helps determine the depth and breadth of the therapeutic relationship, and, therefore, the depth of the therapeutic work. Those of us who do psychotherapy know how awkward the first few sessions with a client can be as a person struggles to become comfortable talking with a complete stranger when there is neither safety nor trust. When things go well, the client learns that her therapist is someone who does not judge her and who can be trusted with sensitive and sometimes embarrassing information.

Helping a client begin to trust the therapist and to feel safe sometimes means being creative. For example, if a client has been abused in a room with a closed door, we may work out our schedules so that we can leave the door to the therapy room cracked open and leave some open time after the session to ensure that the waiting room will be empty. These kinds of actions on the part of the therapist may allow the client to build trust in the therapist and feel that the therapy room can be safe.

The importance of safety and trust in the therapy relationship that is critical in any therapeutic endeavor increases dramatically in the midst of dealing with traumatic events in therapy. Trauma is overwhelming: There is too much affect, too much to take in and no way to protect one's self. The original experience held no safety and supported no trust. Given that the survivors of abuse are re-experiencing a memory in which, often, their perpetrator was a family member or friend, who was supposedly "safe" and "trustworthy," establishing a sense of trust becomes difficult at best. No matter how hard the therapist works to create a different kind of relationship in therapy to minimize the pain of the "reliving" these overwhelming experiences, there often is at least some portion of those feelings that will manifest in the therapy room. This issue becomes a central focus of the therapy between the client and therapist as they work together.

In pre-trauma time, Sue worked to establish a sense of safety and trust in our relationship. During those years, we would have labeled our process together as one in which safety and trust were consciously being built and nurtured. Even during times when Sue made mistakes or there was a simple misunderstanding, Elizabeth could experience that Sue was a trustworthy person as we worked to undo whatever had temporarily threatened the safety and trust we were building.

However, when trauma time descended, there was a shift that became very confusing to both of us. As Elizabeth began to relive the worst of her traumatic experiences, she struggled with a feeling that it was not safe to see Sue and talk with her about her memories and reactions. It seemed logical to Sue that Elizabeth must have experienced some level of safety because she was still coming to therapy at least twice a week and sometimes more. However, Elizabeth did not agree, and reported that the solid foundation of safety was no longer there. During this time, Elizabeth expressed some trust in Sue, but even that waxed and waned with the levels of intensity of the memories recovered.

Talking together while writing this book, we realized we needed to more clearly delineate the difference between safety and trust to accurately describe what was happening between us during trauma time. We have used the metaphor of rock climbing: when a person is rock climbing, she may feel absolute trust in her partner, equipment and training, but at no time is the process of rock climbing considered safe.

We found the same to be true during trauma time. We found that safety was not something that was built, becoming consistently stronger as time went on. No tool was going to implant safety into our experience together. Since the nature of the experiences Elizabeth was reliving were terribly dangerous and experienced as life-threatening, there was no way that Elizabeth could feel safe when she met with Sue to discuss these experiences. However, Elizabeth was able to explain that there was a part of her who knew or at least could hope that Sue was someone she could trust to be with her as she endured these memories and overwhelming emotions attached to them. A true sense of safety left completely while Elizabeth's ability to trust Sue waxed and waned throughout trauma time.

We define Safety in trauma time as:

Having an internal sense that you are free from danger and/or have the resources to reasonably protect yourself, including knowing the potential for danger and how to reasonably avert it.

We define Trust in trauma time as:

Having the belief that someone with you in an unsafe place can be counted on to help and has your best interests in mind.

Another way of delineating these two concepts is to think about Safety as an absolute, and Trust as the relational part of the equation. The question "is therapy/rock climbing a safe experience?" would have to be answered "absolutely not," and no amount of reassurance will make it so. That leads to trust, the relational part of the equation. We can then focus only on the comfort trust might bring: Do you trust your equipment, do you trust your partner to not drop the rope, etc. Getting the right equipment and learning the skills of using that equipment become the basis for making trauma time even tolerable.

Having a history of a trusting relationship and having the therapist working to constantly nourish and maintain that trusting relationship becomes key in making trust possible in the midst of trauma memories. The question becomes: Can the client trust the therapist to be who she needs her to be at any given moment, present during the terrors and complexities of trauma time and available to help as much as possible? When the atmosphere feels overwhelmingly unsafe, can the trust between the client and therapist sustain them enough to maintain a connection and forge ahead?

After we unlinked these two concepts, it became much easier to discuss and understand our experience. When Elizabeth was not in trauma time, safety and trust existed on the same continuum. If Sue acted in ways that increased Elizabeth's trust in her, Elizabeth could experience a sense of safety when she worked with Sue. The longer Elizabeth saw Sue for therapy, the deeper her sense of trust in Sue became and the safer she felt discussing difficult subjects. Once we entered trauma time, safety and trust were no longer linked.

It was confusing when Elizabeth would explain that she did not feel safe in Sue's office, so much so that she had great difficulty getting to the office and then crossing the threshold. It was even more confusing to Sue when Elizabeth began to doubt that she could trust Sue. For Elizabeth, the shift to an experience of no safety and an unreliable sense of trust was both frustrating and very scary.

As the memories wore on and Elizabeth experienced more and more traumatic memories, we entered a final stage that went beyond the Safety/Trust continuum. During this time, Elizabeth explained that she was still coming to therapy because she was desperate, not because she trusted Sue or felt safe with her or in her office. It was a matter of survival. Her thinking was: "It's not safe, I can't trust Sue, but I am so desperate that if I don't come to therapy I won't be able to stop from killing myself."

It's important to note that at the time Sue knew Elizabeth was feeling desperate, was highly suicidal and was struggling to trust her. However, she also still nurtured a belief that there was *some* trust available that she could draw on and that the shared history had some impact on Elizabeth's ability to get to therapy and do what she needed to do. Elizabeth deeply regretted the loss of trust in Sue and berated herself for it. She experienced profound shame that she could not overcome this struggle and return to the experience of trusting Sue.

What was critical, especially as we examined these events in retrospect, was that Sue could respond to Elizabeth in the moment, not try to argue her out of her mistrust, and work with what was available: someone in an abyss of despair, looking for help. Any attempt by Sue to coerce Elizabeth to trust or remind her of our past relationship left Elizabeth feeling very misunderstood and often shamed. Understanding desperation became the point of connection, and the only place of a shared reality. We were left with the moment only, because Elizabeth did not have a reliable history to help her either feel safe with, or trust, Sue.

Connection to other three factors

The Safety/Trust factor is profoundly impacted by our first three main factors, especially during trauma time. As mentioned earlier, Temporary Is Permanent complicates trust building. In a "normal" relationship that is not impacted by trauma, a sense of trust is built over time. That building over time allows both parties to assess the relationship, recognizing what happened in the past and what is happening in the moment.

With Temporary Is Permanent in the mix, that capacity is compromised. There is no history that can be reliably seen, so each interaction in the moment is all that is available, making trust hard to achieve. Even after a session in which Elizabeth was able to trust Sue with strong emotions and terrifying memories – or even good ones – that level of trust did not carry over into the next session because the experience was temporary.

This made both of us very frustrated and confused. Why wasn't our level of trust building with each positive experience? Why couldn't Elizabeth feel safe after Sue had provided a nonjudgmental space for Elizabeth for years? Since everything was temporary, the trust Elizabeth felt toward Sue was reset to a minimum level at each session.

Certainly, the Shame Filter also complicates building trust and the creation of safety. If, in the moment, the words, affect and experience of the relationship are twisted and distorted by the Shame Filter, the ability to assess the wisdom of trusting this person is compromised. The Shame Filter leaves clients doubting their own senses and not accurately "seeing the other rock climber," which makes a dangerous task absolutely terrifying. Sometimes just Sue talking about the lack of safety in the service of trying to help only made Elizabeth's shame more intense, and added the "inability to feel safe" to the "inadequacies" that she had been experiencing.

It became a vicious circle, with shame from the memories feeding shame in the relationship, distorting any attempt to battle the confusion it caused. When Elizabeth struggled with her ability to trust Sue and when she intensely experienced the lack of safety with Sue, she felt ashamed by her reactions. She asked herself often: "Why can't I trust Sue anymore? Why am I so afraid of her? She must hate me and I still go to see her. I am such an idiot."

Once it became clear that Elizabeth was unable to feel safe, Sue struggled with feeling responsible for the loss of the experience of safety in the relationship. She believed deeply in doing what she could to build trust with her clients, knowing how important a trusting relationship is in helping someone to heal from trauma. When even that trust seemed elusive, it was hard for Sue to not feel shame herself in somehow having failed Elizabeth.

Having Suicide Is Always an Option certainly wreaks havoc on any attempts to build trust. Strong suicidal thoughts and feelings are often extremely difficult to share in any relationship and the need to trust the other to hear, understand and not judge is paramount. Obviously, just having those feelings expressed implies that there is little that feels "safe" anywhere. Ideally, speaking of suicidal ideation would demand a level of trust that those thoughts and feelings will be heard empathically, without judgment and with complete acceptance.

It was difficult for Sue to manage her own anxiety about the level of Elizabeth's suicidal ideation when Elizabeth would tell her that coming to see her was not safe and that she didn't know if she could trust her. Even though Sue knew that she herself was trustworthy, and wished that Elizabeth could experience that again, the reality of the absence of a reliable sense of trust meant hearing strong suicidal thoughts especially difficult.

In the following vignettes, we hope to show the continuum of our experiences of safety and trust, the ways in which our connection was evident, the ways we tried to nurture and build whatever safety and trust we had, what it looked like when there was virtually no safety and little trust, what desperation looked like, and ultimately how we came out on the other side of the battle to a place of deep connection. It was anything but a straight line, but to Elizabeth, the over-arching picture went from a place of considerable safety and trust to a precipitous drop in those feelings to an experience where only Elizabeth's feelings of despair and her need to survive were present. Not until the memories faded could Elizabeth return to a place of safety and trust.

Safety fading, trust remaining

Once trauma time began, safety largely disappeared. We had had an established history of trusting each other, which allowed Elizabeth to begin telling and Sue to begin listening to memories. These next vignettes, all from a relatively early period in trauma time, provide a picture of just how tenuous the experience of safety felt, as well as describe ways we used the trust we had already established to enable Elizabeth to share these memories, despite the danger of the prospect.

Elizabeth: Holding hands

When I was with Sue today I talked about how scared I was trying to talk about these new memories. The normal easy conversation between us was replaced by my halting speech. Words got caught in my throat. I settled back in my chair and closed my eyes to tell Sue about an image I had in my mind.

I told her about a young girl who was terrified and hiding. The young girl I visualized was myself. As I was trying to give voice to the girl, Sue knew how difficult it was for me to stay with this image and feel the grip of emotions that the image was generating. When I continued to struggle, Sue asked, "Would you like to hold my hand?" I immediately said yes and imagined this young girl taking Sue's hand in the imagery. I was very surprised when I heard Sue moving her chair. I opened my eyes and saw that Sue had moved closer to me and was holding out her hand for me to take. At first I was shocked that she meant for me to actually hold her hand in the office rather than in the imagery.

I hesitated a bit and then thought that holding Sue's hand would help me continue. I took her hand and she squeezed mine. I leaned back into the chair and again closed my eyes. I had more courage to face what I remembered and what I was experiencing because I had Sue's hand in mine. When I started to falter and hesitate again, Sue squeezed my hand. Sometimes she stroked it. It was very soothing and comforting. I don't know that I could have said as much as I did or experienced the depths of terror and agony I touched without holding hands with her. It helped me experience that Sue was really with me. I didn't feel alone. I felt calmer when I was done exploring this image because having the physical contact with Sue grounded me. I was so glad Sue is not afraid of touching a client. It was very healing and made me feel like I was not alone. I hoped the feeling of trust with Sue would last.

Sue: Whispered terror

We had been in the midst of horrific memories for a while. Today, Elizabeth came in very disturbed. She had remembered a new piece of her story and wanted to tell me, but was obviously in agony trying to do so. I pulled my chair closer, as I often do, and offered my hand. She took it right away but then sat in silence for about 10 minutes before reluctantly beginning her story. Her body was rigid, and it was clear she was re-experiencing a childhood experience of terror. She was unable to speak in full voice. Instead, her story came out in terrified whispers like a child remembering unspeakable horror. I leaned in as far as I could, breaking all kinds of physical boundaries just to be able to hear most of what she was telling me. I responded only occasionally, as she seemed to need just to tell the whole story without a break. She seemed relieved by the end of the session to have told me what she had remembered and nothing much else was said. I was glad she was able to trust me enough to tell that part of her story.

An unknown connection helps Elizabeth hold onto trust

One of the delights of doing therapy is its unpredictability – at least when you believe in entering a session with no preconceived agenda. For us, what could be seen in traditional therapy as an "error in self-disclosure" became a key that opened up our relationship in deeply meaningful ways. At a time when safety had waned and trust was tenuous, a new language became available to us and allowed an immediate deepening in our felt connection with each other and certainly a way to strengthen what trust we had. The following vignettes illustrate discovering this connection and the impact it had on our relationship.

Sue: Music connection

I felt completely drained after today's session. Elizabeth was in the midst of a flood of new memories that have been coming steadily for a month now. When she arrived, she said she needed to sit on the floor. I stayed in my chair, but slightly angled myself toward her. She talked about always having loved music and remembered that she seemed to have a natural talent for whatever instrument she tried. However, there seemed to be a split between her talent and the amount she played. Part of the disconnect lay in the reality of being sleep-deprived most of her teen years, as well as in needing to fight off traumatic memories from her conscious awareness.

In addition, like other things she loved, her abusers found a way to toxify music, making it impossible to use her love for music in any satisfying way or separate it from her abuse. She grieved that she had lost something that might have been soothing to her now and longed in particular for the ability to play the piano. At this point in the story, the tears welled in my eyes without my being able to stop them. She was so close to my personal experience that holds my relationship with music and the piano as pretty much sacrosanct. She quickly picked up on my tears and asked me what they were about. I told her "I can't imagine a life without music," still struggling to keep my tears in check. I disclosed to her my connection to the piano and the importance music had in my life.

I had never shared this with her, but now told her that I have a degree in piano and my "other life" is intimately involved in music. She was suddenly animated. She said over and over again that she had told herself "she's my therapist, not a musician," to keep herself from talking about and sharing music with me. She grinned at me – this was too good to be true! I felt embarrassed by my unusual show of emotion, but also very close to her at that moment. I got it. We shared an emotional and spiritual connection now that we had not known about before.

Elizabeth: Listening together

It was show-and-tell at Sue's today. I brought in a big boom box and a CD containing Jewel's song "Hands." Ever since Sue told me that she has a degree in piano performance, I felt I could probably trust her with the songs that give me strength. She would understand or at least not make fun of me. Even so, it took me a while to play the song for her. I knew she had a music background and that music meant so much to her, but I hadn't felt safe sharing this song. I had to keep reminding myself that Sue would understand why this song is so important to me.

I told her a little bit about the song and then we listened to it together. Her first comment was: "Where did you find this song?" She was clearly touched by it. The song speaks of doing good works even when we don't have much to work with. It speaks of using the power we have and the utmost importance of kindness. It touches me deeply because, despite what the men did to me, I never want to treat others that way. I want kindness to guide my actions – not revenge or an attitude of "I had it bad so you should too." I think Sue shares that value and feels it would be understandable for someone with my history to turn bitter and angry. She understood that my attachment to this song speaks to my need to be kind and put positive energy in the world. Playing the song was more powerful than just talking about these values. Thank God for music.

Sue: Lullabies

I was leaving for vacation in a few days, and Elizabeth had been struggling with finding ways to counter the terrified part of her that believed I wouldn't return, confirming her all-too-present belief that her life has no value. She brought in a book of piano music and wanted me to look over it with her. She was looking for pieces that could be "lullabies" to counter her terror and wanted my help in choosing pieces she could play for herself. I supposed that if I helped her choose pieces that might be soothing it would help her feel safer in my absence. We paged through the whole book slowly and talked about each piece. I picked out a few that seemed to fit the bill, and she marked the ones she would work on while I was gone. In the process we also talked about some of the technical difficulties of each piece and some of the terms used, and commented on favorite composers we shared. It wasn't the typical therapy session, but our connection to each other was palpable and being able to share this particular language in the face of the separation that felt so dangerous was a real blessing.

Actions speak louder than words

As it became clearer to both of us that safety was gone and trust was shaky, there were times when actions better expressed just how hard it was to feel that lack of safety and minimal trust. In the first vignette, Elizabeth showed Sue just how unsafe she felt in her office. The following two vignettes demonstrate how differently brief moments of trust may be experienced by each individual. The third vignette shows how a question meant to support trust can trigger traumatic memories, rendering trust into a toxic experience.

Sue: Tricorder

I have always said that we learn from our clients, but I never expected that would include an insider's view of "Star Trek!" When Elizabeth called about wanting to bring a tricorder to session, I didn't really know what she was talking about. However, from the tone of her voice, I knew it was critically important to her and was another way she was trying to help herself find a way to be in my office.

She came today, hesitating, embarrassed and unable to get all the way into the room. She explained that she wanted to use the tricorder to scan the room for evidence of the men bugging my office. It made sense to me right away. I knew she had childhood experiences of being brainwashed into believing that talking to a therapist was tantamount to killing someone she loved. I knew that her childhood experience taught her that no one is safe, no place is safe.

Here was a concrete way to counter those teachings by taking action to assure herself that my office was a safe enough place. No one was listening and no one knew she was there. We went through my office, pillow by pillow, picture by picture, until there was nothing we hadn't scanned. It felt very serious to me, and we both kept a very focused, business-like tone until the job was completed. When we finished, Elizabeth seemed to relax and we were able to laugh about it.

Sue: Let her sleep?

Had anyone been videotaping the last half of our session today, there might have been some serious questions about my competency. Elizabeth came in with another memory that she was able to tell me about rather quickly, though certainly not painlessly. We spent some time going over it and feeling the impact of this new memory on her overall story. It was not an easy memory to take in. After a long pause, she closed her eyes. It gradually became clear to me that she was actually asleep sitting up in her chair. I debated with myself about waking her. I wasn't at all sure that she might not be embarrassed to discover herself sleeping in session, and I also questioned if she would be angry if I just let her sleep away some of her time with me. In the end, I decided to let her sleep until about 10 minutes before the end of the session. I woke her as gently as I could and explained my decision. She said she felt good about having had that experience with me and to feel like she trusted me enough in that moment to completely let down her guard. Sleep had been so unsafe for her as a child that it was a relief to experience her sharing a traumatic memory and being able to sleep afterwards.

Elizabeth: Lego house – breaking out of the basement

As I did on most nights after Ellen went to bed, I took out my Legos and finished the house I had been building. This time I was building the basement in the house where we were tortured. I made the stairs that led to the basement and the separate torture rooms. The walls were thick and impenetrable. I built the torture tables and closets. I used the Lego figures as the children. It was all there. The basement was inescapable. It freaked me out to build it but I couldn't stop. I used hundreds of Legos. I usually brought the houses and fortresses to show Sue. Last night I didn't know if I could trust Sue enough to bring in this one. It was too graphic for me. It wasn't symbolic of something. It was factual. Still, I decided to bring it into today's session.

I had a very difficult time walking down the hall to Sue's office. When I arrived at the end of the hallway, I hesitated before opening the door. When Sue opened her office door, I couldn't look at her for very long. I walked into her office with a large bag that contained the house with the basement. I sat on her sofa and took the house out of the bag and placed it next to me. Sue brought a small table over and I placed the house on the table. She moved her chair closer.

It was so difficult to talk. I spent 10 to 15 minutes sitting in silence because I could not allow myself to speak of this place of torture and of no escape. My emotions were churning. I became increasingly agitated from the memories and from my inability to express my internal world. Sue tried to help me verbalize what I was feeling. She asked questions about this house. I just couldn't speak. As I sat on the sofa feeling my anger intensify, I realized that there was something I wanted – no, needed – to do. I wanted to destroy this house. I wanted to escape this house and never enter it again.

Without warning I stood up, picked up the house above my head and forcefully smashed it onto the floor. We were both shocked! I thought the house would fracture into three or four pieces but remain largely intact. That's not what happened. Most of the Legos broke apart! There were hundreds of Legos scattered across Sue's office. We looked at the devastation of the shattered house. After the shock of seeing how totally the house was destroyed, I felt a sense of relief and satisfaction. I had destroyed the basement! It was no longer a place I could be taken and tortured until I was broken over and over again. Now the basement was broken.

We sat down amidst the scattered Legos and talked about how fulfilling this experience felt to us both. With 10 minutes left of the session, it was time to clean up. I got on my hands and knees to gather the Legos and put them in the bag. I used a piece of thick paper as a shovel to scoop up all the Legos that had looked like bricks an hour before. Sue and I laughed as we found Legos under chairs and the sofa. We found them under the furniture cushions. How did they get there? We found them in every section and corner of the room.

To be free, finally free of the basement! It was an act of anger that was transformed into an act of freedom. I had no idea when I made this house and brought it into Sue's office that I would impulsively pick it up and, in a controlled rage, destroy it. All of the rage that I could never express was poured into this one act. And it liberated me. I didn't know what this experience would mean in the future. I wasn't sure how the basement would continue to haunt me. But from today, I knew that it would never have the kind of power over me that it had had since high school.

I'm glad I felt safe enough with Sue for her to witness this. She had been helping me dismantle this house for years now. Destroying the basement in such an unexpected dramatic fashion seemed right. There was no doubt in my mind that the basement could never be rebuilt. It was finally gone. And in that moment I was able to regain the trust in Sue that I hadn't been able to feel in a long time.

Terror of connection

It may not seem obvious to someone who is not a trauma survivor to recognize the enormity of the courage required to face overwhelming trauma and find a way to lessen its effect on his or her life. It is a "leap of faith" like few others: In the heat of the work, there is no felt experience of safety. There is a sense of trust that only ebbs and flows. And there is a real potential for an enormous internal backlash if any trust is allowed. The power of the internal battle between the experience of some trust, desperately wanting to believe in that trust while also experiencing the abject terror in risking that trust, is seen in the next vignettes, all of which occurred later in trauma time, when memories were most intense. The courage required to trust in the midst of screaming memories is huge. Elizabeth's "simple" walk down a hall to Sue's office illustrates that courage.

The impact of Temporary Is Permanent also can be seen as Elizabeth struggled to remember Sue's trustworthiness enough to allow herself to speak. The other side of that painful ambivalence is seen in the second vignette, when leaving therapy became the "safest" thing to do. The third vignette shows the agony of the awareness of the lack of trust, when the only feeling is despair. Finally, we provide an example of how Elizabeth acted out the lack of safety and the level of terror in the office.

Elizabeth: Walking the gauntlet

"Just walk into the building, take the elevator to the sixth floor, walk down the hallway and open the door to her office. Come on, Elizabeth, you've done this hundreds of times already. There is no danger here. You can do this."

Despite my pep talk, the same pep talk I had given myself for years, my pulse was racing. I was sweating profusely and I felt a little dizzy. The worst part of this walk to Sue's office was the long narrow hallway on the sixth floor that has doors on both sides. When there was daylight outside, I could walk down the hallway without the panic that some of the men were waiting behind the office doors to kidnap me and punish me for telling the secrets. It was easy to see that someone was not waiting on the other side of the frosted glass door fronts when the offices were illuminated.

Today, the hallway between the elevator and Sue's office became "the gauntlet." The offices were dark inside. Ten doors on the left and eight doors on the right of the hallway were all opportunities for attack. Today, a walk that usually took 30 seconds expanded to 15 minutes. Another person got off the elevator with me. Sometimes when this happened, my embarrassment at stopping in the middle of the hallway allowed me to keep moving and dampened the terror that prevented movement toward Sue's office. Not today. Today, I stopped halfway down the hallway, leaned against a wall and looked out the hallway window. The person in the elevator asked if I needed assistance. I wanted to tell about the gauntlet. I wanted to shout: "Yes, I need help. Get me to safety. Don't leave me here alone." Instead, I told her that I felt a little dizzy and needed to pause for a minute.

Once I arrived at Sue's door, I froze as I reached for the doorknob. "This is not a good idea. I don't want to face these things. I need Sue's help. I can't do this alone. But I can't trust her. But I need to try." I turned the handle and walked into the waiting room. Sue opened the door and greeted me. I forced myself to walk into her office. Then I asked myself, "Now what do I do? Sit down? Hide behind the chair near the door? Pace? Sit across the room? Stand in the middle of the room? Desperation, terror, exhaustion and shame determine what I do after getting into the office. How will I ever feel safe again?"

Sue: Not coming anymore

Last night I received a very disturbing call from Elizabeth. She left a brief message that said she was not coming in anymore and "just wanted to let me know." That was it – no explanation, no details. My anxiety rose as I tried to figure out what had happened to cause this sudden turn of events. Elizabeth had talked often about her ambivalence in coming to sessions – especially when her memories were at full tilt and she had trouble believing that I could both tolerate hearing them and still care about her once a story was told. I reviewed our last session, but couldn't remember any major misunderstandings that might have led her to want to quit so abruptly. I decided to avoid making guesses on the phone and called her back right away and told her I was sorry to hear her message, I really wanted to understand it and I expected to see her today at her regular time. I hoped that would be enough to get her in the door so we could talk about it and begin to figure this out.

She came in on time, but was obviously angry. She talked about her extreme frustration with the therapy process but couldn't clearly articulate what she really wants. She was feeling "out of it, confused and unfocused." She said she had called "to protect me" and really believed that I "would be relieved." I spent some time trying to reassure her that I had been anything but relieved to get her message. The truth was, it had stayed with me all night and I was tremendously relieved to see her walk through the door to my office. It was hard for her to believe me, and it took a lot of conversation for her to even consider the possibility that I cared for her.

I finished the session feeling exhausted, once again realizing the fragility of the hold we had on this relationship and just how tenuous was the trust between us, while at the same time recognizing that it was all I had to battle this crisis. I guessed I could feel good about the fact that she trusted me enough to tell me how hopeless she felt. Small compensation.

Sue: Silence speaks of terror

Sometimes Elizabeth entered my office looking like a terrified child. This was one of those days. She barely spoke, and could offer me no eye contact. She sank into her chair, and remained silent for 20 minutes. She let me know that she had something she wanted to talk about, but despaired that she would not be able to say anything. She said there was so much that she'd planned to say and was profoundly disappointed in herself to be unable to say anything. She argued with herself that she should be able to trust me enough to tell me what she needed to, but found it overwhelming. I tried to understand with her what was making it so hard to speak.

We spent the session feeling the frustration and self-shaming of wanting so much to share some piece of her story and being so completely terrified to do so. The clinician in her was horrified that she wasn't able to trust me enough in those moments to talk. She cried that she knew I wasn't out to get her, she knew I cared about her, that I had never abused her, shamed her or cut her off, but all that intellectual understanding couldn't successfully do battle with the terror underneath that knowing.

There wasn't much I could say. She knew our history and could speak it to me. All I could do was try to sit with the frustration of doing battle with such powerful, terrorized parts of her that simply could not even begin to trust me in this moment. I hoped that being with that terror would help rebuild some of the shaking sense of trust she was experiencing.

Of course, it was frustrating for me too. I wanted to say, "Come on, trust me! Really, nothing bad will happen!" There was also an internal question for myself about whether I was doing something wrong. Was there anything else I could be doing to help her do what she wanted to do? What could I do differently to help her trust me enough? I wanted to remind her of all we had gone through at this point but knew that would only further shame her. That was exactly the dilemma. She did know who I was, and who we had been together, and it wasn't helping her at all. She had all the information and could remember our relationship. But she couldn't trust it.

Elizabeth: Hiding from the men

I'd been doing things that I never thought I would do. I was ashamed and embarrassed. I *was* desperate. First, I had to fight myself to get into Sue's office. Then when I made myself enter her office I often was stopped at the door. That happened again this morning. I couldn't get my feet to move. When I finally could move this morning, I could get only to the chair closet to the door. I hid behind a fucking chair. I had always worried that Sue would think I was acting or that I was a freak. Regardless of what Sue thought, I felt like a freak. I was a grown woman and I was hiding behind a chair.

Did I ever hide behind a chair when I was a child? I'm not sure. I don't remember ever doing that. Yet, here I was, hiding behind chairs. I couldn't help it. I was terrified in Sue's office. I tried to trust her. I guess I trusted her enough to get myself into her office. Trusting Sue could get me only so far. No matter how little or much I trusted her, her office was not safe. Talking about what happened wasn't safe. Sue might have been standing in front of me, but I was terrified that the men would burst through the door and take me away. Maybe they were already in her office. All these thoughts and terrifying flashbacks overwhelmed me at the door to her office. My only response was to squeeze behind the chair and hope that I won't taken away again to be tortured.

Today, as I was hiding behind the chair, Sue stood near me and talked to me very gently and softly. Slowly she convinced me that the men weren't there with us and that I could walk into the room without fear of harm. Sue told me that she would not let the men take me away and she would not let them into her office. She reminded me that the men were very old now and that they could not overwhelm me the way they could when I was a child.

I needed to hear all of that to be able to come out from behind the chair. I felt so stupid. It was hard to look at Sue because I felt so ashamed by my behavior. We talked about that once I sat down in a chair. Sue did not say anything that was judgmental. She did not shame me or make my embarrassment any worse. I wished Sue's office felt as safe as it used to. It was so dangerous to go and see her. I just hope the men don't kill me when I'm there.

Trust becomes consistent again

When the trauma memories stopped, we began to experience the return of the steady trust we had in each other in pre-trauma time. Elizabeth was also beginning to feel that pre-trauma time sense of safety. During this period we revisited the possibility of writing a book together. But before we could address this possibility, we focused on a large collage that Elizabeth made in sessions over the course of several months.

Elizabeth: Talking about writing the book again

I never thought that we would have this discussion again. I had felt like such an idiot since suggesting that Sue and I write a book together. We hadn't talked about it in years. I wasn't sure if she even remembered that I had mentioned it years ago. But these past six months had felt different than the previous several years. I had moved to a place of being able to trust Sue again. Her office felt safe for me again. We were sharing on a different level. I no longer sat in silence, struggling to speak for most of the session. There was camaraderie between us that had been gone for years.

We had both learned so much about doing therapy with someone healing from trauma, we thought recounting our unique experience might be helpful to others. We had both worked with lots of people who had survived many kinds of trauma. Sue had been a therapist for a long time and she also had expressed the sentiment that she has learned a lot from me. I certainly learned a lot from her. I thought we could use our story to illustrate how a powerful relationship between a client and a therapist is what creates healing. I felt very strongly that our relationship is what saved me.

For a long time I didn't know if it was wise to trust Sue. I missed the connection we'd built over many years. I didn't know if it would ever return. Over these past several years, I had moments when I regretted mentioning that I thought we should write a book together. I was hoping she wouldn't bring it up because I would have told her absolutely not. But somehow we'd weathered all of this turmoil. We'd made our way back to each other. This experience saved me. It gave me my life back.

I wanted the chance to tell this story. I was so glad that Sue hadn't forgotten about writing a book. She seemed pleased that I asked again and said that she had never forgotten about it but also thought that we would never be able to attempt it because too many things happened between us. Sue had a lot of questions and fears about trying to change the nature of our relationship from client and therapist to co-authors. I believed we could do it. Sue wanted to talk a lot more about it once I was ready to stop therapy. I felt ready to move on—well, I'd never feel totally ready. I felt restless, though, as if I needed the time I spent with Sue to pursue other things. I needed to reclaim my life and discover what my life was after remembering so much torture and suffering and cruelty. Maybe a part of reclaiming my strength and reclaiming my relationship with Sue was to write this book together about the painful and phenomenal experience between us.

Sue: Collage

Elizabeth suggested doing a collage to help us "finish" this trauma work, a process that took several months and resulted in a complicated, multilayered collage. Elizabeth supplied all the materials, but we put each piece on together during our sessions. The first layer had unspeakable pictures of torture, pain and humiliation. The board was covered with these images. Once that was finished, Elizabeth brought in pictures of musical instruments, which she placed all over the pictures of abuse. Finally, after some deliberation, she brought in red and yellow tissue paper and made "fire" all over the poster. Once finished, there was no evidence of the first layer.

It was such a mixed experience doing this with Elizabeth: At one level, we could both see what was happening on that poster board and the enormous weight of meaning it held. At the same time, we were sitting on the sofa, armed with scissors and glue sticks, looking like a couple of campers on a rainy day! We both knew, however, that it was the symbolic end to our work together and therefore was enormously important.

Sue: Ritual to end

We finished the collage last week with all its layers and stages. There was palpable relief between us. It was as if the trauma literally has been put to rest on that huge poster board. Both of us had expressed the need to do something with it and began talking today about what that would look like. We ended up realizing we needed to burn the poster together, and that required a trip to the lakefront and a barbeque grill. It was important to walk there together and release it to the fire and the air. She asked that I write a poem about it, and I did, right after our session:

THE JOURNEY

We have traveled this path

like two prisoners

On a forced march,

captives of an unnamed army,

following orders from ancient places.

We began as strangers

but with each weary step

have come to know each other

and fall in line.

We have guided and cajoled one another,

our voices under the radar

of our captors' ears.

We have plotted as we traveled—

escapes thwarted,

plans shattered,

we have blamed each other for our misfortunes.

Begging to know how long, how far,

we have looked up to ascertain the master plan

from constellations we have never understood.

We sought out our prison guard,

and found him numb, mute and unreachable.

We have tried to sing,

but found screams and sobs

easier on the throat.

Exhaustion has traveled with us.

But now, there are whispers of armistice

on distant hills.

Labored negotiations made,

land occupied, now freed.

And so, through battered vegetation

we walk with quickened step

over newly reclaimed territory

to this shore.

It is here where we finally come to rest,

these last miles walked of our own accord –

the army deserted.

It is at this shore

that we come to remember our journey,

look back at the seemingly aimless path

that has led us here.

Here we will unburden

this untold story to the air.

Here we will render its images

to light and warmth.

Here we reclaim the voice to sing the melody,

and the hands to play the notes

that will transform this journey

into the song

we have both sought.

CHAPTER 8

From Post-trauma to Co-writers

Post-trauma time

AS CAN BE SEEN near the end of each chapter, there was another part of our therapy that followed trauma time. As new memories slowed and eventually halted, we began to re-group and focus on recovering from all that Elizabeth's trauma had meant to her. This period looked very different from the bulk of "trauma time." During those six months or so, there was a qualitative change in our relationship, seen in the waning power of the four factors that we have been describing.

Without Temporary Is Permanent at the forefront, we began to look back on our relationship in trauma time and experience a shared understanding of what we had done and who we had been to each other. Elizabeth was able once again to take in the full picture of our relationship, remembering who Sue had been to her and putting into a broader context what the trauma time therapy had meant. We could reliably depend on the history of our knowing, even if parts of that story were experienced differently by each of us.

The constant presence of suicidal thoughts also dissipated during post-trauma time. Rather than expending considerable time and energy convincing herself to live, Elizabeth began to focus on trying to create a future for herself that had to include the horrific story she now remembered more fully. Elizabeth knew she needed to find meaning for her life, a spiritual core and an identity that was different from that of victim, and that became an important part of post-trauma time therapy.

As the Shame Filter began to lift, we were again able to weather any misunderstandings that arose during therapy sessions. We were far less anxious that we might step into a minefield and lose our newly reclaimed connection. Gradually, Elizabeth was able to believe again that Sue cared about her, saw her strengths and hadn't judged her for the horrific abuse she endured. Sue could make a comment or ask a question without worrying that the Shame Filter would get in the way, and Elizabeth felt a renewed ability to hear those questions or comments without the distortion of the Shame Filter. With the luxury of being able to look back on our time together without The Shame Filter between us, we were able to see where we had been and where we were now.

The dilemma of safety and trust also shifted during post-trauma time. The waning of the memories and the danger inherent in them allowed for a safer experience and more trust between us as we began to look back with clearer eyes on where we had been. In retrospect, both of us could see that the commitment Sue had made, along with Elizabeth's ability to keep coming amidst unfathomable pain and fear, had gotten us to a new place. We saw just how hard we had worked to recover from our disconnections and saw that our relationship had thrived despite those challenges. We knew in a very profound way that we could trust each other.

Although the eight years of trauma time contributed to a relationship that felt far deeper than the first few years of pre-trauma time, in some ways post-trauma time revisited our pre-trauma time relationship. We were both relieved as it became clear we were done with the tyranny of new memories that had constantly disrupted the battered relationship that we shared. We could relax just a little bit more, coming up for air after a very long time in the trenches. We rediscovered our comfort and enjoyment of each other. We could have deep discussions about the meaning of life, reading Frankel during the beginning of this period. It was a time of regrouping and shifting to a consideration of life after trauma therapy. Elizabeth began to acknowledge the enormity of what we had experienced together as she looked ahead to reinvesting in and reinventing her life.

It would be misleading, however, to conclude Elizabeth had no further traumatic reactions. She did. However, her capacity to manage what she was experiencing and to know her immediate reactions were predicated on her history was dramatically different. This shift also was visible in the contact that we had outside of the therapy office. During trauma time,

Elizabeth often needed to call Sue, and regular phone contact was the norm. During post-trauma time, this occurred much less frequently. The tenor of those calls also changed. Elizabeth was far less dependent on Sue and far more able to manage her reactions by herself.

Perhaps one example might be helpful: Near Halloween during this period, Elizabeth was suddenly approached by a man in a long robe and mask, reminiscent of some of her abusers. She experienced a traumatic reaction and was shaken by the incident. She called Sue and left a message explaining what had happened. However, part of the message was that she was OK and didn't need a call back, which would not have been the case in trauma time.

Part of the work during this time also included looking back on our trauma time with the new lens of post-trauma time. As we reviewed our experiences together with clearer vision, we began to see the value in our newfound understanding of all that we had been through together. The idea of writing this book resurfaced and that became the focus of our therapy for some time.

We have devoted this book to an exploration of our experiences as therapist and client. What may also be of some interest is a brief look at our individual experiences as co-writers. What follows are our final thoughts looking back on the writing process itself as we transitioned from our therapeutic relationship to one of colleagues and co-writers.

Sue: Experience of transition to writing and experience writing it
In the introduction to this book, I outlined my concerns, anxieties and hopes for the writing process and the care we took to address them before we began this part of our time together. Despite the work we did to give each other time and patience to form a different kind of relationship, it was sometimes difficult for me to become comfortable in my new role with Elizabeth. I felt awkward and worried that it might not work out.

Despite a break between the end of our therapy and the beginning of our new relationship, we began the writing project still a bit raw. Not all wounds had healed, and Elizabeth's trauma history was still very much with her. We could not deny our history together and begin our relationship as new friends might normally do. There was no handy road map.

The tenderness I felt toward Elizabeth often made me fearful that I might injure her again. At the same time, along with being intellectually fascinated by what we were reconstructing, I struggled with the need to look at my failings again. The new revelations, new criticisms and mutual re-examinations were difficult and quelled any temptation for me to rewrite our history. However, we survived, just like we had survived so much during our therapy. This time we had the clarity of post-trauma time to help us see the forest for the trees and our relationship ultimately got us through. It was only a few months into our work together that I began to trust that the relationship that had survived 12 years of therapy would carry us through the co-writing period.

There were many surprises for me, as well. As seen in many of our vignettes, our understanding of the ongoing process was not always mutual. That disparity continued as we deconstructed our work together to find a language that would encapsulate all we wanted to articulate regarding what had worked well for us and what had caused us so much confusion. We had many places of mutual understanding, but surprisingly, many places where we understood things quite disparately. In certain situations, things I had forgotten stood out to Elizabeth as the most important moment. A comment I made that felt like an error to me became a key for her in trusting me. Things I was sure were central didn't feel very important to her. I wished every therapist could have the experience of what we jokingly called the longest termination process in history!

As humbling as the process was for me, it was also extremely gratifying. I loved being able to ask the question "what the heck happened when . . . " and then be able to help each other figure out the explanation. We could "stop action" on a particularly confusing moment and spend whatever time we needed to unravel the confusion. It was a fascinating process. Elizabeth and I had talked a great deal about how things felt during our work together, but no amount of therapy hours can get it all. In the process of writing, I learned even more about her experience and understood much more clearly about the impact of my relationship with her. I was sometimes surprised to learn the depth of Elizabeth's pain in certain situations that may not have been expressed at the time. The experience was fascinating, humbling and awe-inspiring.

The review process was also very helpful for my personal growth. I had to acknowledge the places I got stuck, the places my own need for self-protection took over and left Elizabeth out and the places where I couldn't or wouldn't see something. I saw clearly the limits of my fatigue in the process. Those very real aspects of me were part of our writing together, and my impatience with the limitations were seen and accepted. The healing went both ways.

There was another significant bonus for me. As much as a career working with trauma survivors forced me to see the evil in the world, knowing Elizabeth gave me a picture of the incredible capacity to survive, and indeed, to thrive. Her courage, tenacity and spirit were remarkable. I got to watch up close her enormous capacity to plow through unspeakable trauma to get to a place of healing. It is such a corny thing to say, but truly, it was an honor.

Elizabeth: Transition to writing book, and experience writing it

Although I didn't doubt my decision to end our therapy, I had concerns about the nature of starting this new relationship with Sue as co-writers. I began the process with a lot of clarity about avoiding any hint that we were still in a therapist/client role. In retrospect, I occasionally kept a more rigid boundary than was necessary, but I wanted this new stage to be completely separate from our old way of relating. At the beginning of the writing process, I was sometimes frustrated when we talked and we initially seemed unable to make sense of things. Ultimately, however, it was both surprising and intellectually fascinating to explore these misunderstandings and very different experiences with each other. Rather than saying "that was intense," we were able to stay with the confusion until we reached a place of some understanding. I felt we were discovering ways of talking about this that were not pathologizing and that my clinical beliefs were being reinforced. I felt I had new ways of understanding my own clients as well that came directly from these conversations.

The process of writing this book also was very painful for me. As we were writing about the pain that I endured and the healing that occurred because of Sue's commitment and relationship with me, I relived all those dark memories. Although I believed in the importance of writing this book and enjoyed much of the process, it was also hard to "look forward" to working on the book when it meant opening myself up to the horrific experiences that had crippled me for so many years. This unbalanced the dynamic between us. Sue was able to forge ahead with topics and vignettes. She had more energy and focus and was not triggered as much by the material. I had to fight through layers of trauma still within me. I struggled with fatigue, an inability to concentrate on the writing and shame when my mind and body wouldn't cooperate with my still strong belief in the work.

I also had a series of health problems that dramatically interrupted our work. I had so hoped that the end of the trauma work would mean fewer physical symptoms, but it did not. I suffered continued bouts of seasonal affective disorder, battled cancer and won and had several other illnesses that significantly slowed me down. While certainly my life is much better since our therapy, I still have to work hard to maintain my life through ongoing meditation, tai chi, diet and exercise.

CHAPTER 9

Final Clinical Thoughts

AS WE APPROACHED the process of writing this book, organizing all that we had experienced together was daunting. We believe that structuring our discussion around four major factors allowed us to develop a framework that would help the reader conceptualize the big picture. However, there are other important beliefs worth noting that weave in and out of these four factors.

Remember: The relationship is central

First, the centrality of the relationship cannot be overstated. This statement may sound simplistic, but it is not. Making the relationship central means that any preconceived ideas the therapist had about "trauma therapy" or what happened during the last session must be set aside to be in the moment with the client. It means largely leaving tools, techniques and theories at the door. It means paying attention not only to what the client says but also to what those words mean about your relationship.

You are expected to be a healer—not a "psychologist" or "therapist" or "clinician" and, as such, you are on sacred ground. We ask a lot of trauma survivors to come into a room with a stranger, sit down, close the door and then be vulnerable enough to talk about a traumatic event. The therapist must respect the risks that the client takes in a beginning therapeutic relationship and work constantly to nurture a relationship that can support the work. Survivors know all too well the dangers of relationships that aren't reliable, that can't be talked about, that can't be trusted and that can't be made safe enough. These experiences are likely to be directly and indirectly, consciously or unconsciously, front and center in the work you are doing, regardless of whether you are talking directly about the relationship. The impact of how well the relationship is tended will be a huge part of the healing from the traumatic relationships that brought the client to therapy. Healing takes a relationship that is deep, strong, solid, honest, genuine and loving. Nothing less will do.

Get comfortable with fewer boundaries

Putting the relationship first can mean sometimes leaving the comfort and relative safety of hierarchical boundaries. The concept of boundary issues is used to describe the difficulty some people have in finding a comfortable distance in their social relationships owing to a history of relational abuse of some kind. The term describes the dilemma of being caught between powerful needs to connect, and on the other hand, a terror of the connection that triggers a "push back" from any connection. Well-defined roles for both the therapist and the client are an important aspect of what makes therapy work. The challenge of establishing boundaries in therapy with trauma survivors is incorporating an authentic relationship into the therapy and knowing where the boundaries need to be for that particular therapy relationship.

Part of our success was our ability to stretch the boundaries of traditional therapeutic relationships to accommodate the trauma that was being relived, and remembered between us. This didn't mean we were socializing outside therapy, meeting in the park or over coffee or sharing details of Sue's life. It meant that there might be a phone call on a holiday, a totem carried on vacation and, most importantly, a level of honesty in the conversation that precluded any hiding behind a professional role. For example, if Sue wasn't as emotionally available as she normally was because of something in her own life, sharing that information, even if it was technically "self-disclosure" that went beyond normal bounds, was essential.

The place of theoretical constructs

There certainly are many theoretical frameworks available to help understand what goes on during the process of therapy. They may be of some help to you in organizing your thoughts about what is occurring. However, our strongest advice is to leave your theories at the door as much as possible so you can be present with your client. It is our belief that labels, theories, roles, strategies, treatment goals and techniques carry a risk that they will only serve to insulate you from what is actually going on in the relationship and the very individual story that is unfolding before you. Each client is different, and it is critical to hear him/her without any preconceived notions. Elizabeth was adamant that she did not need a clinician who would spend valuable session time trying to slot her into a theory, offering possible "meanings" for what she was feeling or providing an explanation of what her behavior might actually indicate. She was very clear that when Sue colored with her, built Lego houses or listened to songs Elizabeth played for her, Sue entered her world without barriers of theory, labels or techniques. Those experiences were critical in her healing. This can be scary for clinicians whose training is often focused on diagnosis and treatment planning rather than working with helping the client find her own path. As difficult as it may seem, we still believe our clients just don't fit into any boxes, and we shouldn't try to put them there.

Symptoms as adaptations

The focus on the individual story of the client leads to seeing "symptoms" as unique adaptations to the client's actual experiences that either disrupted or prevented some piece of "normal" development. This is unlike some symptoms of major depression, for example, that may or may not have anything to do with reality. Viewing symptoms as adaptations avoids any tendency to attach negative labels that may lead to a diagnosis that is helpful to no one, fosters a much more empathic and less blaming stance from the therapist, and helps create a more self-empathic experience for the client. For example, a client who frequently cancels sessions might be labeled as "resistant to therapy," but if understood in the context of a trauma survivor coping with the high risks of forming a relationship an entirely different stance can be taken. Not coming to session becomes an important part of the dialogue between the therapist and client.

Be self-aware

Much more important than any theoretical understanding for the therapist is awareness of herself as a person in the therapy room. Please keep a constant eye on your internal experience as the therapist and be clear about the source of the feelings there. There are so many feelings and so many details that occur in the course of a therapy session that it is imperative that you constantly work on your own responses. It will be pretty hard not to get triggered somewhere along the process, so it becomes your responsibility as a healer to know your own triggers and be vigilant about owning them when they show themselves. Exactly how you manage this is up to you, but it must be something that allows you to be able to be honest with yourself. It must include a nonjudgmental space for your own exploration. Classes, meditation or your own therapy are all possibilities. We believe this also means making a commitment to having some kind of supervision. For Sue, a trusted group of peers, with whom she had been working for over 20 years, provided immeasurable help. It's critical to be able to find a safe place to air your own responses so you can go into session with a clear head.

Be in the present

This overworked phrase has a great deal of merit for the therapist dealing with the vast uncertainties and confusion of being with someone in the midst of trauma memories. Our sometimes-reliable markers of "signs of progress" can be woefully lacking in the midst of the muck. As therapists, we may find ourselves confused when a client who has made us aware of her sense of trust in us suddenly declares that we are completely untrustworthy. Remembering that survivors had to learn to accurately and almost instantly "read" the intentions and motives of another person to stay safe helps explain the sudden change of stance for the client, which can feel like a rollercoaster for the therapist. As our chapter on Safety and Trust illustrated, there is a battle being waged, and the most important thing you can do (just like in meditation) is to "keep your seat." Stay with the mess and uncertainty. Stay with the inconsistency and lack of linear progress. Stay with the anguish and the shame that can seep and stay in every crevice of your client, office and sometimes even yourself. Trust that your genuine and present self will allow you to provide the safe, stable and nonjudgmental space that will lead to your clients' ultimate healing.

Client's strengths

By now it's probably clear to the reader that being in the midst of trauma memories can challenge everything we expect from the process of therapy. Seeing a client trying to cope with horrific memories, understand the present relationship through a murky shame filter, fight off impulses of suicide and struggle to maintain any sense of trust in the therapy relationship make it difficult to remember the strengths the client showed before the trauma memories began. For the client, it can be difficult, if not impossible, to feel or access these abilities. For the therapist, it can also be frustrating to "know" the client's abilities but witness the client's inability to access those resources.

This becomes a delicate dilemma for the therapist. For us, Sue's reminding Elizabeth of the "Old Elizabeth" that Sue still remembered was, at certain times, a critical part of the healing. At other times, to Elizabeth, reminding her of those qualities shamed her, and triggered more despair that a part of her was experienced as irretrievably gone. Whether the therapist chooses to remind the client of her strengths at any given moment, it is still imperative that the therapist maintain a sense of who that person is without in any way discounting the core capacities of that client. For Sue, trusting that, despite the enormity of her handicap, Elizabeth had the resources to survive gave Sue hope and energy to continue even when Elizabeth herself had little or no hope.

Make a commitment

Beyond everything else, we believe an undying sense of commitment to your client is absolutely critical. It feels like a marriage vow, without the possibility of divorce. The process is often exhausting and can deplete every resource you have. To do this work, you have to have the life situation, personal energy and patience to hang in there for the long haul. It will mean extra phone calls, extra sessions, lots of tissues and endless empathy. Not every therapy will last 12 years, but they often last many years; thus, working with a survivor of trauma means making a huge commitment. The damage done when therapists decide they've had enough, can't give the client any more, aren't skilled enough or have some other reason for terminating with a trauma survivor is incalculable. Don't do it. That said, using the "it takes a village" model supports seeking additional resources. For us, having Ann as a back-up therapist was extremely helpful to both Sue and Elizabeth. For others, a therapy group or a support group might help share the burden.

Final thoughts

There were many layers of deep satisfaction for both of us in writing this book. Although we did not completely share our clinical orientations, they were close enough and Sue was flexible enough that our most deeply held beliefs were illustrated and confirmed. Those beliefs were expanded to include this new language and further supported by the very intense and significant experience we had shared.

Elizabeth: Words to survivors

My words to fellow survivors are these: Try with all your might never to give up on yourself. When you find a clinician who seems able to sit with you as you cry, grieve, rage, come unglued and cling to her because the terror overwhelms any ability to function, do what you can to stay with her. It will be ugly and messy and absolutely 100 percent terrifying. Do it anyway. This is the way out. We were crushed at the hands of others, often by those we trusted or who were supposed to protect us and nurture us. For many of us, when these crimes were committed against us, there was no escape. Now there is.

But the door to freedom leads to the same process in which the abuse is embedded: trusting another to hold us, accept our pain, not run away and not take advantage of our vulnerability. This process is not for the faint of heart. It takes courage initially to walk into a therapist's office to ask for help, and it takes enormous amounts of courage to keep returning. We quickly learn that this process is not a straight line to relief.

We have friends who experienced immediate benefits working with a skilled clinician. That's not how it is for us. For us this journey worsens before we find bits of relief. We must live through weeks, months and sometimes (as was my journey) years of hopelessness before there is a breakthrough. Even then the first breakthrough can be so small – enough breathing room to go to a party, or maybe just out of the house or to work for a few hours. How about the surprise of the first session without sobbing?

A part of me wishes that after such an intense and long healing process, my life had totally turned around – that I had boundless energy and was filled with a happiness and contentment most of the time. The truth isn't as straightforward as that. I think many survivors of trauma will be relieved to hear that I still struggle–to get good sleep, to find ways to relax. My body, mind and soul were formed with the background of extreme abuse and neglect. Sue helped me build other internal structures so that the effects of the abuse aren't as debilitating. I have my good days and bad days. My relationship with Sue helped the good days be more plentiful and the bad days not to last as long. I am able to embrace pain in a way that allows for growth in connection rather than isolation and aloneness.

Ongoing healing and struggling don't diminish the importance of my time working with Sue. Those years allowed me to reclaim my life and discover parts of it for the first time. She helped me uncover my past. Knowing the past and understanding it allowed me to claim my own life. Since my time with Sue, my motives have become clearer. I understand my choices and reactions in a deeper way. I can be open to more of life – and not as scared. There are times when I actually feel a deep happiness and contentment. But I am scarred and will carry those scars to my grave. I hope that these scars now allow me to be more open to the world, more open to the suffering of others and less willing to judge.

Our final words together

Finally, we hope that the years we spent together, in and out of therapy, can be of some use to you, the reader, survivor or healer. This process has meant that each of us, in her own way, had to set aside personal fears of what others might think of our experiences, our clinical conclusions and our personal failings to do what we agreed to do together. We have offered our most honest and thoughtful retelling of what was a life-changing experience for both of us. As clinicians, we believe there can be no greater "high" than seeing someone you have sat with for years–someone you have come to love–begin to come alive again. This is a story of courage and, ultimately, triumph. We have shared at a level that is rare in this world, and we treasure that experience. It is our wish that our story can inspire you to build therapeutic relationships in and out of the therapy office that will help heal the brokenness that we see in our offices, in ourselves and in our world.